Paragraphs Plus: From Ideas to Paragraphs to Essays

Paragraphs Plus: From Ideas to Paragraphs to Essays

C. Jeriel Howard
Northeastern Illinois University

Richard Francis Tracz
Oakton Community College

Scott, Foresman/Little, Brown College Division
Scott, Foresman and Company
Glenview, Illinois   Boston   London

Library of Congress Cataloging in Publication Data

Howard, C. Jeriel, 1939–
    Paragraphs plus: from ideas to paragraphs to essays/C. Jeriel Howard, Richard
Francis Tracz.
      p.   cm.
    Includes index.
    ISBN 0-673-39727-0
    1. English language—Rhetoric.   I. Tracz, Richard Francis.
II. Title.
PE1408.H68515 1987
808′ .042—dc 19

                        87-22747
                            CIP

1 2 3 4 5 6 7 8 9 10 — RRC — 93 92 91 90 89 88 87

Printed in the United States of America

Source Lines

    Pages 89–90: Excerpt from Richard M. Currant, *The Lincoln Nobody Knows*,
McGraw-Hill, 1958.
    Pages 90–91: Excerpt from Stephen Birmingham, "A Bore Watcher's Guide,"
Sports Illustrated, 1960.
    Page 115: Excerpt from E. B. White, *Letters of E. B. White*, Harper and Row,
1976.
    Pages 124–125: Excerpt from Paul Gallico: "A Large Number of Persons," *The
Saturday Evening Post*, September 5, 1931.

Acknowledgments

    Pages 13–14: Free writing exercise by Marjorie Kellison. Copyright © 1988 by
Marjorie Kellison. Used by permission.
    Pages 18–19: Journal entries by Louis Escobar. Copyright © 1988 by Louis
Escobar. Used by permission.

Acknowledgments continue on p. 215.

Preface

Paragraphs Plus offers basic writing students carefully paced instruction that moves from the developing and focusing of ideas to the writing of paragraphs and, finally, essays. Beginning with the first unit on the writing process and continuing throughout the text, students are constantly asked to think about the writing act and to become increasingly aware of themselves as writers.

Part I introduces students to the processes of writing and includes assignments that ask them to think and write about writing. We have found this type of reinforcement activity that turns back upon the writing process to be especially helpful with basic writers. Revision is also treated in Part I as a part of the writing process and not, as is too often the case, as a final chapter in the text, too late to be useful. Students can see in this early part of the book how revision works and can begin to apply these techniques for revision to their own writings from the very beginning of the course.

Part II is a thorough presentation of the rhetoric of the paragraph with an emphasis on its generative nature. Within the framework of the paragraph, students can learn about the standard forms of rhetorical development. The instructor may easily move to the smaller unit of the sentence and concentrate upon grammar and style or to the larger structure of the complete essay, of which the paragraph is a kind of microcosm. We have provided examples and exercises that permit students to see the growth of short, skeletal paragraphs as writers develop them into various levels of complexity. Throughout Part II students are shown schematics for paragraphs in process as well as for completed paragraphs. We have found that these schematics serve as very useful mapping devices for basic writers. This paragraph section contains numerous examples from professional writers and from our own students. Assignments within each chapter are designed to move from the simple to the complex. The larger movement within the entire Part II is from personal experience writing to traditional expository prose.

Part III shows students the logical movement from paragraphs to essays and stresses the similarity in rhetorical development of the two. Assignments frequently ask students to take paragraph-long pieces that they developed in Part II and expand them to essay length. This section also contains information on writing introductions and conclusions. Each chapter in this part contains both a rough draft and a finished essay by one of our students, giving further reinforcement to the text's emphasis on revision as a part of the process.

The organization of the text permits a great deal of flexibility according to an instructor's perception of the needs and abilities of a specific class. For example, instruction may first involve work only with the paragraph (Part II) and then move to the essay (Part III), or it may loop from one to the other. For instance, an instructor might teach the rhetorical concepts of the illustration paragraph in II and then move directly to III to show how the illustration essay is simply an expanded version of the same set of concepts.

We thank the many individuals who contributed toward the concept and the development of the text. We are especially grateful to our own students whose work appears throughout the text and who often gave us suggestions for writing topics that now appear as assignments in the book. We specifically thank the following students: Cedric Brown, John Boras, Kimberly Croteau, Louis Escobar, Elizabeth Franks, Susan Hastie, John Hareas, Marjorie Kellison, Maryellyn Kroschel, Valerie Laffoon, Carolynn Monroe, Earle Prieske, Vanessa Rodgers, Melissa Strayhorn, and Shelton Williams.

We want to thank our colleagues Steven A. Dolgin, David Koenig, Marilee McGowan, Karen Muskat, Shelly Samuels, and Sylvia Stathakis. They have frequently made suggestions that helped us sharpen an assignment or better illustrate a concept.

The comments that we received from our reviewers were especially valuable to us, frequently causing us to rethink certain assignments, examples, or explanations. We wish to thank the following individuals for their conscientious reading of our manuscript and for their helpful suggestions: Helen C. Covington, North Harris County College; Ed Lotto, Lehigh University; Cecilia Macheski, LaGuardia Community College; Beatrice

Mendez-Egle, Pan American College; Randall Popken, Tarleton State University; Audrey Roth, Miami Dade Community College; David Skwire, Cuyahoga Community College; Harvey S. Weiner, LaGuardia Community College; and Joe Opiela, our editor in Boston.

And, of course, we remain grateful to Pretza and Herr Schmitz for their companionship and love.

C. Jeriel Howard
Richard Francis Tracz

Contents

Part II: The Paragraph   61

Part III: The Essay   161

Paragraphs Plus:
From Ideas to
Paragraphs to Essays

The Writing Process

Thinking About Writing

Getting Ready to Write

Drafting and Revising

C H A P T E R

1 Thinking About Writing

You have probably witnessed the following scene many times, maybe even been a part of it yourself.

A class, not necessarily even an English class, has been having a lively discussion about a topic. Almost everyone in the class has taken part. Although opinions have differed widely and there have even been a couple of angry exchanges among class members, everyone has stood his or her ground. And every student seems to have several good, logical reasons for the position that he or she is taking.

Suddenly, the teacher's voice rises above the students' voices: "Well, everyone certainly has a strong opinion on today's topic. Now, I want you to use your ideas to write a short essay defending your position. Be certain to make clear the various reasons that support your ideas."

The classroom that was so active just moments before is now quiet. Some students take out paper and begin to write. Others take out paper and just stare at it. And some take the rest of class time rearranging the books on top of their desks, sharpening their pencils (for the third and fourth times), or doing any other task than the one assigned: writing.

What has happened in this situation? Why are students who were moments before so filled with ideas and so eager to share them now so reluctant to write about those same ideas? Just why is writing such a threatening activity?

The illustration that opens this chapter was recently discussed with a group of writing students at the beginning of the course. Here are some of their comments:

Louis: Somehow my ideas always sound so good when I talk about them, but they just don't look the same way when I have to write them down. They sometimes sound silly then.

Marge: I don't feel that we are being graded when we're just talking about ideas together in class. When the teacher asks us to write something down and turn it in, I know we're going to be graded. I freeze.

Ken: My handwriting is so bad that I hate to write stuff out for anyone else to read. I talk fine, but I can't even read my own writing sometimes.

Deborah: I'm such a poor speller. When I write, I spend most of my time looking up words in the dictionary. When I talk, I don't have to know how to spell the words.

Eric: Writing just always seems so much more formal. When I talk, I never feel that it's final. I can always reword something or take it back if it doesn't work. When I write, it always looks so final. And if I make a change, then my paper is messy and doesn't look good.

Lydia: I always made bad grades on my writing in high school. I guess I'm still afraid. I can still see those red marks everywhere.

Regina: When we talk, our ideas always just seem to fall in place somehow. When I have to write, I never know what idea to use to begin my writing and how to arrange the rest of the ideas. My teacher always seems to find something wrong with the way I've put it all together.

Exercise 1

Discuss the illustration at the beginning of this chapter and the students' comments with your own classmates. What similar and different attitudes to the same situation can you find in your own classroom?

Writing and talking are different. In a way, Eric is right: Writing is more formal; you can't take it back. When you are talking, especially in a classroom discussion, you are organizing many of your ideas as you go along. When you write, you need to have done some organizing of your ideas ahead of time. When you talk, you can watch your audience to see if they are agreeing or disagreeing with you. When you write, you do not have the benefit of this feedback. Since you will not be present to say "but I really mean such and such" when your reader is reading, you must be certain to say exactly what you mean when you write.

The difficulty in writing, though, is not just as simple as the difference between talking and writing. If you look back at the students' comments, you will see that several of them are related to faulty ideas about writing and about the writing process. Look for a moment at some of the faulty assumptions about writing:

1. *Everything should be written in one sitting from start to finish. Later changes should be simply to correct spelling and punctuation problems.* Most writers usually don't work this way. As you will later learn in this text, an essay has many different parts. Sometimes you don't think about those parts or write about them in the order that they will appear in your final version. Also, the first (and sometimes even the first two or three) versions of a piece of writing will typically undergo numerous changes before you are ready to produce a final version. These changes will probably include some spelling and punctuation corrections, but they will also include moving parts of sentences or paragraphs around, changing individual words, deleting some words or phrases that are no longer needed, and providing transitions to improve the flow from one sentence or paragraph to the next.

2. *Correct grammar is the most important aspect of good writing.* Correct grammar is certainly important, but it is not necessarily the most important part of your writing. Your ideas—what you say and how you say them—are very important to the success of your writing. Granted, a paper that is filled with grammar errors will not be successful. Similarly, though, a paper that is completely correct but that says almost nothing at all (or says the same thing again and again for two or three pages) will also not be successful. If you are

too concerned about being correct in the early stages of your writing, you, like Marge, will probably freeze. Your ideas just won't come. You should learn to get your ideas down in your early stages of writing and to be attentive to grammar, punctuation, and mechanics in the later stages.

3. *If you have something to write, get started writing. Don't waste time figuring out a plan ahead of time. Let your ideas develop as you write. One idea will lead naturally to another.* This plan is a fine one if you realize that what you are doing at this stage is only a very preliminary draft. If this is true, then getting your ideas down is the important goal; you can, indeed, sort them later. This plan is not a valid one if you allow yourself no time to rethink and revise the parts of your essay. The order in which ideas pop into your head is not necessarily the best order to present them in your writing.

4. *The final essay is what really matters in your writing. That is what the teacher is going to grade.* This idea is not a sound one because your final draft is always a product of the various steps (thinking, prewriting, revising, etc.) of the writing process and does not exist by itself. If you have not carefully done the other parts of the writing process, the chances are quite good that your finished product will be faulty in its development or its organization. Writing teachers are becoming more and more interested in what you do at each of the various steps of the writing process, not just with what you turn in as a final product. Many of these teachers, then, evaluate your work on such activities as prewriting, drafting, and revising with just as much attention as they evaluate your final essay.

The parts of the writing process will be discussed in some detail in the second and third chapters of this text. For now, think of those parts in the following broad categories: *finding and limiting a subject, gathering ideas about the subject, organizing those ideas, drafting and revising,* and *preparing the final paper.*

The same students who discussed the differences between talking and writing at the beginning of this chapter were given a brief questionnaire asking them to indicate which of the areas mentioned above gave them the greatest problems. Students were asked to mark the one category that frustrated them the most when they had to write and to indicate briefly why. Here is a summary of their responses:

Attitudes Toward Writing

The steps of the writing process have been broken into five categories below. Place an *X* beside the category that most concerns you when you write. Briefly indicate why you have problems with this category.

Finding and Limiting a Subject   **18%**

_____can't think of anything interesting to say

_____never have anything exciting to write about

_____assigned topics are always so boring

Gathering Ideas about the Subject   **23%**

_____can never think of examples

_____say everything I have to say in less than a page

_____most of what I think about is so obvious that everyone already knows it

Organizing Ideas   **34%**

_____never know how to begin

_____keep coming back to the same idea and saying it over and over again

_____don't know which ideas to put in what order

_____get confused between organizing and paragraphing

_____can't move smoothly from one part to another

_____my endings always sound like a sermon

Drafting and Revising   **20%**

_____can never find anything to change in my early drafts

_____don't know when to expand or when to condense

_____make very few changes at all from draft to final

_____revising is mostly checking for grammar and spelling

Preparing the Final Paper   **5%**

_____never enough time

_____bothered by having to be neat

_____still want to make changes, even at last minute

Exercise 2

Although you will learn much more about each stage of the writing process in the second chapter, you already have some general ideas about the five categories listed above. Discuss with your classmates which of these five seem to give you the most trouble. (Your teacher might even wish to calculate class percentages and compare them with those given above.) Why do you think you are bothered so much by the category you marked? How might you go about making yourself more comfortable with this aspect of writing?

Thinking about writing is often just as important as writing. One task this text will ask you to do again and again is to think about writing. The more you think about it, the more you will be able to identify both your strengths and your weaknesses.

For instance, you might not have a problem with *writing* so much as you have a problem with *thinking of something interesting to say*. If so, that is only one aspect of writing. The chances are rather good that you don't have a problem with *organizing*; that is, you don't have a problem with all aspects of organizing. You may just have trouble writing an interesting opening paragraph. You need not be frustrated by the entire writing process; you need only work on your one problem area. Once you know where your problem is, you can work on it. But think about it first.

Exercise 3

You didn't really think you were going to get all the way through this first chapter without writing, did you? Think for a moment about the single most difficult writing assignment you have ever had. What made the assignment so difficult? Maybe the topic itself, maybe the time you had to work, maybe your fear of a final grade? What could have been changed to make the assignment an easier one? Perhaps an opportunity to refocus the topic slightly, perhaps more time to develop your finished paper, or perhaps not having the paper count so much toward your final grade? Write a couple of paragraphs in which you describe this writing project and what made it so difficult and then offer some suggestions for how it might have been made easier.

C H A P T E R

2 Getting Ready to Write

Stop and think for a moment. For almost everything that you do in your life, you allow some time to get ready. You get ready to celebrate a special occasion. You get ready before you ask your boss for a few days off. Even if you are going to play tennis with some friends for the afternoon, you get ready. You decide what clothes to wear. You decide what equipment you need, find it, and check it over. You remember that you must take some suntan cream and sunglasses. And, you allow time for the drive or walk from your house to the tennis courts. All of this is getting ready, preparing for the main event.

Unfortunately, most people allow themselves too little time to get ready to write. But getting ready to write is just as important as writing itself. If you take time to get ready, both physically and mentally, your completed writing task will inevitably be better.

GETTING READY PHYSICALLY

Remember that in the last chapter we discussed the importance of *thinking* about writing. Now, you should begin thinking about the physical aspects of writing, that is, where you write and what equipment you use. If you are uncomfortable with either your writing environment or your writing equipment, you will not do your best.

Granted, there are times when your writing environment is controlled for you. For instance, you have little control over your environment when you have to write at your desk in a classroom filled with other students. However, you do most of your writing outside of the classroom and in places where you *can* control the environment.

Remember your past experience with writing. Where have you been the most comfortable? Some people don't write well at all if anyone else is present, even if the room itself is quiet. These people, perhaps, don't like to write even in a library; instead, they prefer the privacy of their own bedrooms or dens where no one else is present. Other people can't stand to write in such isolation and prefer to be among people even if they are not talking to them. In which group do you belong?

Think about some other situations that are a part of the writing environment. Which of the following best reflect your writing world?

writing at a desk
writing on a pad on your lap

having absolute quiet
having soft music in the background

working in a completely clear area
working in an area that is surrounded by books and notes

being able to look outside through a window
facing a wall with no outside view at all

These are just a few of the options that you might consider as you plan your ideal writing environment. Remember that you can make a choice. Your objective is to find the place where you are the most comfortable.

Selecting the writing equipment that best serves your needs is another part of controlling the physical aspect of writing. Once you have determined where you write best, begin to think about the equipment you use.

Individuals respond differently to the various writing tools. Some people literally do their thinking at the typewriter. These people don't do especially well when they have to write something by hand. Other people prefer to write at least their first drafts by hand. They feel more in control of the work this way. But even among these people there are differences. Some of them like to write on ruled notebook paper, some on blank pages of white paper, and some on yellow legal pads. Some always write with ballpoint pen; others write with a pencil. Even some people who use computers find that they like to write out much of their material by hand before putting it into the computer.

What about your own writing habits? Which of the writing tools best suits you? Do some of them make you tighten up and become less creative? Once you have determined which tools you like, stay with them. The more comfortable you are with your writing tools, the more comfortable you will be with your writing.

Once you are confident with the choices you have made regarding the physical nature of writing, you will save yourself a great deal of time preparing for a writing task. No longer will you waste time moving from one writing spot to another. You will already know where you want to write. And you will not have to waste time figuring out whether you need ruled notebook paper or a yellow legal pad. You will know.

Exercise 1

Write a paragraph or two in which you discuss the physical environment where you are the most comfortable writing. Describe that environment and then briefly try to explain why you think you work well in it.

Exercise 2

Write a paragraph or two in which you discuss the physical environment where you are the most uncomfortable writing. After you have described the environment, try to explain why you feel uncomfortable writing in it.

Exercise 3

Write a paragraph or two in which you discuss the writing equipment that you are the most comfortable using. Try to explain why you especially like to write with this specific equipment.

Exercise 4

Write a paragraph or two in which you discuss the writing equipment that you are the most uncomfortable using. Try to explain why this equipment makes you feel uncomfortable and how using it negatively affects your writing.

GETTING READY MENTALLY

Getting ready mentally involves thinking about what you are going to write, thinking before you write. If you think about your project before you begin to write, you will have more control over the topic and over the details that you use to support it. You will probably want to change or expand some of your ideas as the project develops, but you should begin with a good idea of the direction you want to go.

Developing this sense of direction involves four different activities: finding a topic, limiting the topic, gathering information, and organizing information about the topic. Each of these activities should be a part of your mental preparation for writing.

Finding a Topic

Good writing usually comes about as the result of good topics, and good topics are most often those about which the writer feels strongly. If you are excited about a writing topic, your excitement will show. And if you are bored, your boredom will show. If you have a topic that interests you, then the chances become greater that you will interest your reader with it.

Even if your instructor gives you a topic, you often have the opportunity to individualize it by bringing your own personality or interest to the subject. For instance, suppose your instructor asks you to write about the differences between living in a large city and living in a small town. If you are a sociology major, you might focus your paper on the differences in housing opportunities in the two places. If you are a parent, you might focus on the differences in the quality of education. If you are planning to be a teacher, you might examine the schools and job opportunities in both locations. The point is to select an aspect of the topic that interests you.

Actually, students seem to have more difficulty with finding a writing topic when they are left completely on their own. In those instances, "I can't think of anything to write about" is a common complaint. One way to avoid this problem is to begin now by thinking about a large number of topics for your future writing.

Keep a List of Your Interests.   Set aside a page in your notebook for a list of topics that you feel you could write about. The list need not be formal. It is just a record of the broad topics that you are thinking about. Don't worry if some of the topics on the list overlap. If you begin to get several topics that are related—all on the broad theme of rock music or rock musicians, for instance—you are moving toward identifying a major area of interest that you will want to explore. Remember, too, that this list is never finished. You should add to it as you think of other ideas. The more ideas you have on this list, the more possibilities you have when you actually need to select a topic for your own writing.

Here is the list that one student recently prepared:

Interest List

- – summer softball
- – rock music
- – home computers
- – my record collection
- – psychology
- – my job at the radio station
- – trip to London
- – my grandfather
- – my pet dog
- – Pete's old car
- – dancing
- – talking on the phone

This list was just the beginning for that student. Already, though, you can see some common ideas developing. Just from this list of items, it is obvious that the student is interested in several aspects of music.

Exercise 5

Begin your own interest list. It can be quite simple at this stage. Simply make a list of ten or twelve broad topics about which you could write.

Practice Free Writing. Free writing gives you the opportunity to explore many ideas that may be lurking in your mind. When you practice free writing, you shouldn't worry too much about grammar, punctuation, or spelling. And don't worry if you wander around from one topic to another. Simply write for a specified period of time (usually twenty or thirty minutes) every day. Write all of the allotted time. Don't look up and daydream. Write whatever comes to your mind. If you can't think of anything to write, begin with something such as, "I'm bored today and just can't seem to think of anything to write." Keep writing that sentence over and over, and suddenly you will find yourself spinning off in another direction. That is, you will have thought of something to say.

Just doing *one* or *two* free writing exercises is not going to help you a great deal. If you free write regularly, however, you will begin to find some common ideas that keep appearing in almost every writing activity. These common ideas can serve as guides to special areas of interest, areas that you might wish to examine more closely in a structured essay.

Here is Marge's first free writing:

I don't know much about this free writing stuff, but we're supposed to write for twenty minutes so here goes. I guess I could tell you about what I did last night after I got off work. It wasn't anything very dramatic, but at least it beat going home at 9 o'clock and studying. I got off work at 8 and had planned to go home, but then Rick had car trouble and couldn't pick me up as we had planned. I had to ride the bus home, and was that ever a trip. I had not been on a city bus in three or four years. It was packed because everybody was getting off work at about the same time, and I've never seen so many strange people. My friends think I am an unusual person, but I'll tell you that I was the most "normal" looking one on that bus. The others ranged from drunks who hadn't shaved or bathed in weeks to a bag lady in an old, red sweater that still had a tattered Neiman-Marcus label to three leather types in as much black and so many chains that you couldn't believe it. I actually became so interested in trying to listen in on everyone's conversation that I missed my bus stop and had to walk back eight blocks. My twenty minute time is up now, maybe I'll pick up here tomorrow and tell you what these people were talking about.

Notice how Marge's writing simply flows in a rather natural pattern, as if she were telling her experience to a friend. As a matter of fact, Marge later used this piece as a basis for two different writing assignments. When she had to write a paragraph describing a significant personal experience, she discussed how her initial fear turned to curiosity during the bus ride. When she had to develop an essay of classification, she wrote a paper on the different character types she had observed on the bus.

Exercise 6

Do your first free writing exercise. Simply write about anything you wish for twenty minutes. Don't stop; force yourself to continue writing until the time is up. You should make a point to do these exercises on a regular basis.

Limiting a Topic

Interesting writing almost always treats a very limited or focused aspect of a broader topic. If you try to do too much in your writing, to cover too broad a topic, you will write only about generalities or about ideas already familiar to your reader. By selecting a very limited part of your topic to examine, you can develop those details that will make your writing interesting.

While you are in the process of thinking about your topic, you are also in the process of limiting that topic. For many writers, the two tasks—finding and limiting—are so closely connected that they go hand in hand. As a beginning writer, though, you might work more effectively if you think of the two tasks separately.

Once you have decided upon a general area for your writing, you need to think about ways you might limit that topic according to length, time, and purpose (for other aspects of limiting the topic, see pages 64–66).

Generally, you have an idea how long the piece of writing is to be before you start. You may know, for example, that your teacher expects you to write between three and five pages or that your term paper must be at least eight pages long. Knowing the intended length of the writing helps you make some decisions about limiting your topic. If you are writing a paper on the war on drugs, you know that you can't cover everything you might like—an overview of drug use, how drugs are obtained, the dangers of drug use to society, how drug use might be controlled—in three to five pages. You might limit your topic to one that could be handled in the given length by writing only about problems with drugs in your immediate neighborhood. Or you might argue against the use of drugs by dramatically retelling the experience of a friend of yours whose life has been ruined by drugs.

If you are asked to write about the one person whom you most admire, perhaps your grandfather, don't try to tell everything about your grandfather in three pages. Focus instead on the one time when you were just five years old and he took you Christmas shopping and stopped by a drugstore and bought you your first real chocolate malt. The point is to focus on a limited aspect of your topic. Narrowing your topic this way helps you to find details that go beyond the ordinary or the clichéd. You will avoid such general sentences as *my grandfather was a really fine man.* Instead, you will have focused sentences such as *I still remember the two of us drinking our malts and how he tried to teach me to sip through a straw without making slurping noises and how I kept blowing bubbles into my malt instead.*

Another concern that you have as you are limiting your topic is the amount of time you have to work on it. If you are assigned a paper that is due in the next day or two, you obviously have less time to work on it than you would if it were due in two weeks. Some of your ideas for developing a topic may require that you go to the library for background reading, talk with other people to get their views, or do any of several other time-consuming activities. You must think about the time these will take. If you have the time to do them and to write your paper, fine. Otherwise, you will have to restrict your efforts to the time that you have. If you are writing a paper arguing that Little League baseball should be abolished, it would be good to get some ideas from your own Little League coach. But if he has moved to another city and you would have to write him and then wait for his reply, you probably don't have enough time. The point here is to be realistic; don't plan more work for yourself than you can possibly do in the time that you have.

As you think about limiting your topic, you will find it useful to consider your purpose for writing. What is its intent? What do you want to accomplish? Most writing can be analyzed according to purpose and placed into one of the conventional categories: to entertain, to inform, or to persuade. Once you have thought about what you want your writing to accomplish, you can focus your topic to fit that purpose. Suppose you are writing about the general topic of sailboating and your purpose is to entertain. You might focus on one sailboating party that you had last summer, select the interesting incidents, and relate them to your reader. If your purpose is to inform your reader about sailboating, you might explain the basic parts of the sailboat and how each works. If you want to persuade your reader to take up sailboating, you would discuss the reasons that you find sailboating a splendid form of recreation and persuade your reader to consider it for himself or herself.

Exercise 7

For this exercise, select one of the following general topics: cars, clothes, friends, music, movies.

1. Assume that you are going to write a three to five page paper on your topic and that your finished paper is due in two days. Briefly explain what you would try to accomplish in that space.
2. Now, assume that you are writing a ten to twelve page paper about the same topic and that it is due in two weeks. What additional aspects of your topic might you cover in the expanded length? How might you use the extra time to develop your topic further?
3. What is your purpose in writing the paper you have just described? How might you refocus your topic so it would fit the other two purposes discussed in this chapter?

Gathering Information for a Topic

Once you have limited your topic, you need to gather some information about it. Taking time to think about what you are going to say (the details that you are going to use to develop your topic) will help you to decide if this is a good topic for you. How many times have you started to write about something and after a half page or so discovered you really had nothing to say? Remember, too, that you may change your topic as you gather details. Some ideas that you had planned to include may now seem unimportant, and some points that you had not thought about earlier may now seem quite important.

You have three sources available to help you gather information for your topic: yourself, your peers, and professional sources.

Yourself as Source.   You have picked your topic and you have done a reasonable amount of thinking about it. You are, in many instances, already your own best source of information about your topic. What you need to do is to formalize your ideas, that is, put them down in some written form so you can "see" what they really are.

One way to do this, of course, is simply to jot down your ideas as they occur to you. At the very top of a sheet of paper, list the topic you are writing about. Keep that paper with you and jot down ideas as you think of them. You don't need to write your ideas down in complete sentences or, for that matter, in any particular form. Just put them on paper so you won't forget them. You may not even be thinking about your paper when suddenly an idea will pop into your head. Write it down. This random set of ideas will become quite useful to you at a later stage of the writing process when you begin to organize your paper.

A more structured way to see what you are thinking is to keep a journal. You recall that one way to find a topic of interest is to free write. In free writing, you let your mind have free range. You provide no limits at all. Journal writing is more focused than that. When you are writing a journal, you have a topic and you force yourself to think about and write about that topic.

A good way to make journal writing work for you is to give yourself time for several different journal writings about the same topic, ideally spread out over several days. In this way, you let your mind explore various possibilities of the topic and you will probably go deeper and deeper into the topic as you continue your journals.

While Louis was working on an assigment explaining how he saw himself ten years into the future, he wrote the three following journal entries:

October 3

I have always wanted to be a lawyer and so I guess that's the way I see myself ten years down the road. Since I was just a teenager, I have been interested in the way the law works. I guess I was very influenced about that time by Mr. Lawrence who was a lawyer and lived just across the street from us. He always looked so important when he left for work every morning with his briefcase and all. When I got a little older, he used to let me come to his office with him on Saturday while he researched some case. I remember being impressed with all of the books in his study.

I guess another reason I want to be a lawyer is so I can feel that I am helping people. There are so many people in this world who don't seem to get what they deserve. If I can help some of them, then I'll be happy.

In addition to being a lawyer ten years from now, I want to have a nice house with a wife and two or three children. I think all of this will make me happy.

October 5

The more I thought about how I see myself ten years from now, the more I thought about how the really important thing was to be happy. I guess for me to be happy I need to have a healthy, loving family, enough money to live the good life, and some respect from my community. I can't imagine that I would be happy if I didn't have a family to love. I come from a very large and loving family where we are always hugging and telling each other how much we like each other. I want that for me too. I guess I am old-fashioned, but I see me and my wife sitting in front of a fireplace and our children playing just behind us.

Of course I know that it is going to take some money to buy the house with that fireplace and that it is going to take more money to buy food, clothes, and other things that my wife and children need. I don't think I am ever going to be one to be greedy about money, but I certainly want to be comfortable in the way I live. Although we are a large and happy family, I know that we don't always have enough money for everything that everyone wants. I want my own family ten years from now to have everything it wants. But I know I'll have to work hard to make that dream happen.

If everything else like the good family and enough money comes along, then the only other thing I see for me ten years ahead is being someone that people in the neighborhood respect. I guess I'm going back to Mr. Lawrence again because I remember how everyone always talked about what a wonderful man he was.

October 6

After I went to bed last night, I lay awake thinking some more about what I wanted to be like ten years from now. I guess I had never really slowed myself down and thought about a question like that until I had to do this writing assignment. In a way, it is all kind of frightening. There is just so much that I have to do between now and then if I'm going to be the kind of mature, responsible adult that I want to be.

For one thing, I have to learn to settle down and take more responsibility for myself and my own actions. Probably the most important thing for me is to become a successful husband and father and to be able to care for my family in a way that will make us all proud. If I'm going to do something like that, I need to begin taking more control of my life right now. It's too easy for me now to blame my parents or someone else when the world doesn't go right. Just last night I got upset at my mother because she wanted me to help clean out the basement when I wanted to go out and play basketball with some friends.

I don't think an adult has to be someone who is all work and no play. That kind of person is extremely boring. As I think about it now, the adults I most admire are the ones who work extremely hard at their jobs but who are also able to let their hair down, to relax and have a good time when that's the right thing to do. I guess for now I need to learn when it's time to play and when it's time to work. That may be a first step toward becoming the kind of person I eventually want to be.

Exercise 8

Carefully reread the three entries that Louis wrote as he gathered ideas for his paper. Notice how each entry is different from the other two. But also notice how each has important information about Louis' topic. What are some of the common ideas among these three entries? Make a list of the ideas in these journals that Louis might want to use as he writes his final paper.

Exercise 9

Select one of the topics given below for your own practice session with journal writing:

1. how you see yourself ten years from now
2. the single incident from your past that has most affected your present
3. the greatest social problem facing your neighborhood or city

Write at least three journal entries for your topic at three different times, ideally at least a day apart. Plan either to write for a specified time, perhaps thirty minutes, for each entry or for a designated length, perhaps two pages. Save the journal entries that you prepare for this assignment. You will use them when you begin to work on Exercise 11, page 24.

Peers as Sources. You seldom need to write in isolation. Remember that your classmates are writing too and that they may be just as frustrated about their topics as you are about yours. If you talk with them about your mutual writing task, you can probably help one another come up with some ideas.

Even if you and your classmates are not writing on the same topic, you will often find that they have some useful ideas about your topic. Get to know several people in your class; talk to them before and after class. Tell them what you are writing about and ask them about their topics, too. Soon you will be hearing statements such as, "If I were writing it, I would be certain to mention...." or "Why don't you begin by describing ...?" Jot down some of these hints. You will find them useful as you gather more information for your paper.

If you and your classmates are working on the same general topic, then you might use some of the techniques of *brainstorming*. Brainstorming is a problem-solving technique that is frequently used in business. For brainstorming, a group of people are brought together to discuss a single topic. There is no leader of the group and there is no rule as to how the discussion should go. Everyone simply presents his or her ideas about the issue at hand. In this process, mini-debates frequently develop over some of the issues. Some ideas are good and are kept; others are inappropriate and are discarded. But as you listen to all of the ideas, you will find some useful ones for your own paper.

Professionals as Sources. Don't forget that around you on your campus or at your work you have many professionals, individuals with unique experiences and training in particular areas. If you talk with them about your writing project, you will often pick up very valuable ideas that you can include. If you are writing a paper on the importance of a twenty-two-year-old college student's thinking seriously about his or her retirement, you can be certain that your college's accounting or business law teacher has some important ideas. If you are writing about problems of teen-aged drinking, you might talk with someone in the psychology department. And don't forget that the people you work with and the people you see almost every day in your neighborhood are also professionals in certain areas. Consult them if you feel they might be helpful.

Organizing the Information

Once you have gathered some information for your writing, you must begin to think about organizing that information. Later in this book, you will learn several methods for developing your essay, but all of these methods are generally based on three common ways to organize material: *organization by importance*, *organization by time*, and *organization by space*. The kind of information you have will usually dictate the kind of organization you use.

Organization by Importance. A frequently used organizational scheme arranges ideas by order of importance. You may arrange your ideas in a movement from the most important to the least important or from the least important to the most important. The plan that you select is, again, usually dictated by the kind of material you have and also by your purpose.

If your major objective is to inform your reader, you will probably organize in a way that allows you to move from the most important ideas to the least important. You know that some readers have a tendency to read the first part of a report much more carefully than they do the last part. When your most important ideas are at the beginning of your writing, you can be more certain that your readers will read them.

If the purpose of your writing is to convince your reader to take some action—write a letter of complaint to the city council, join you on a picket line, send $25 to a particular charity—you should save your strongest arguments for the end of your essay. In this way, your best and most dramatic ideas come just before you make your appeal, before you ask your reader to do something.

Organization by Time. Certain types of writing virtually demand organization by time. If you are telling a story about what happened to you over the weekend, for example, you arrange your ideas by time. What happened to you Saturday morning? Saturday afternoon? Saturday evening? Sunday morning? Sunday afternoon? Sunday evening? Similarly, if you are telling someone else what happened in a movie, on a television program, or in a book, you arrange your material by time. And if you are writing to give someone directions or instructions, you group your ideas into time patterns: *first you do this, next you do that, and finally you do something else.*

Most writing that is organized by time is arranged so that it moves from the past to the present; that is, it moves forward. For certain types of writing, though, you might find it useful to move backward in time. This movement is especially useful when you are examining the historical background of a topic. For instance, if you are writing a paper in which you examine the deterioration of public transportation in your city, you might begin with the most recent incident that will support your ideas and then move consistently backward in time until you come to the point where the deterioration actually began.

Organization by Space. If your purpose is to describe something, then you will probably organize your information spatially. That is, you arrange the objects you are describing to show how they exist in the space they occupy and their relationship to other objects around them.

When you are organizing according to space, you might think of yourself, the writer, as a movie camera looking at the total scene. As you think of the way that camera would move to take in the scene, arrange the movement of your writing accordingly. The most typical patterns of movement are these:

left-to-right/right-to-left
top-to-bottom/bottom-to-top
near-to-far/far-to-near
large-to-small/small-to-large
clockwise/counterclockwise

The system of movement that you select will be determined by what you are describing. If the dominant focus of your description is on the height of an object, you will obviously move either from top to bottom or bottom to top. If you are describing something that requires you to turn your own head from left to right or right to left to look at it, then that is the movement you would use in your writing. If you wish to catch the dominant impression of something (maybe the yellowness of your cousin's room), you would probably begin with the largest, most dominant sights (her bright yellow walls) and move to the smallest items (the vase of yellow flowers beside her bed).

The important thing to remember about organizing material by space is to be consistent in your movement pattern. Don't jump around from one pattern to another.

Exercise 10

Look back at the journal entries that Louis wrote (pages 18–19) and at your own work in Exercise 8. Which pattern of organization would you recommend that Louis use for his finished essay? Why?

Exercise 11

Now look at the three journal entries that you wrote for Exercise 9 (page 20). What pattern of organization would be most effective for your own essay? Once you have determined a pattern of organization, list the major ideas as you would include them to fit into that pattern.

C H A P T E R

3

Drafting and Revising

Up to this point, you have been involved with prewriting activities. You have selected a general topic, narrowed that topic, and gathered and organized (at least in your mind) some ideas for it. Now you are ready to try out some of those ideas on paper. You are ready to write your first draft to see if your ideas really have "something to say."

Think of writing as a part of the process of discovery. The more you write about a particular topic, the more you come to know about that topic. Don't think that the ideas you put down in your first draft are necessarily your final ones. You will probably revise and refine those ideas just as you will revise and refine your own prose in subsequent drafts.

If you have written some journal entries about your topic, you have, in a way, already done some extremely rough drafts, but they have been fragmented, written at different times about different parts of your topic. Now it is time for you to bring all of those different parts together into one piece. Your first rough draft should give you the opportunity to put your collective ideas down on paper so you can then evaluate them more carefully.

When you write your first draft, you should try to accomplish the following goals:

Put all of your ideas from beginning to ending down in writing.
Keep in mind the general organizational pattern scheme that you thought about as you initially sorted out the ideas you wanted to use in your writing.
Try to make your first draft approximately the same length that you envision for your final paper.

Remember that your objective in writing the first draft is to get all of your ideas down so you can evaluate them. Some matters should not bother you at this stage:

Don't be overly concerned about the correctness of your grammar, spelling, or punctuation right now; you should not be careless, of course, but don't let an intense concern for correctness get in the way of putting your ideas down in some kind of order.

Don't be especially concerned with format, and use whatever kind of writing paper and writing instrument you are the most comfortable with at this stage.

For an example of a rough draft, see Carolynn Monroe's paper on pages 52–53.

After you have written the first draft of your paper, you are ready to begin the revision process. This process involves just what its name implies, revising or editing what you have already written. Revision is not simply rewriting your first draft into a clean format without crossouts so you can turn it in to your instructor.

The revision process can actually be divided into three broad areas: *organization and development*, *style*, and *grammar and mechanics*. Some writers are able to revise their work by looking at all three things at the same time. As a beginning editor, you will probably do better work if you go through your paper three separate times, looking at one particular area each time. Remember that as you revise your paper, you may wish to make additional drafts of it. Sometimes you can make changes simply by crossing out parts of your writing or by adding other parts. But when your changes become extensive, you should probably write out a new draft, just as you did the first one, so you can see what you have composed as a complete piece of writing.

REVISING FOR ORGANIZATION AND DEVELOPMENT

Read your paper through once to examine its organization and development. First, check to see that you have consistently followed one of the plans of organization that you learned in the previous chapter. Do your ideas follow a definite movement according to importance, time, or space? Next, see if you have provided satisfactory transitions from one part of your writing to another. Remember that as a writer you are responsible for giving your reader guidelines to help him or her understand the relationship of the various parts of your composition. Assist your reader when you are moving from one idea to another by using appropriate signal words and phrases (see pages 80–85).

After checking that your writing has a definite organizational pattern, you need to make sure that you have developed all of its parts adequately. A typical problem here is the failure to provide sufficient details to make your writing interesting and/or informative. Too often, an early piece of writing looks like a series of topic sentences, each waiting to have something else said about it.

Exercise 1

Here is a sample paragraph taken from a student's first draft. Following that paragraph are several sentences which the student later added to the paragraph. Determine where those detail sentences belong and rewrite the paragraph to position them correctly.

On a typical Saturday I like to sleep late and then to just hang around with some of my friends for most of the afternoon. I don't like to have anything to do until at least noon so I don't have to get out of bed too early. During the afternoon my friends and I will go to a shopping mall or sometimes just stay at home and listen to music together.

_____ I just can't stand the idea of setting a alarm clock for Saturday morning.
_____ We walk around the mall and window shop since no one has enough money to really buy anything.
_____ About mid-afternoon we go in the coffee shop and have a hamburger and something to drink.
_____ Even if I wake up by about 9 o'clock, I don't like to have to get up that early.

_____ I often just stay in bed, half asleep, and listen to the Saturday morning sounds.

_____ We usually sit there eating, drinking, and mostly talking for an hour or more.

_____ I often hear my mother and father talking, and sometimes I can hear my little sister playing with the girl next door.

_____ But I am never more than half awake and the sounds just all sort of merge with my sleep.

_____ Finally, we usually stop in at the record store and look at the latest things out.

_____ Usually by about 11 o'clock I am wide enough awake that I get up and take my shower and begin the day.

_____ If one of us has money to buy a record, we all talk it over and make the purchase a group decision.

_____ I can't think of spending Saturday any other way than this.

REVISING FOR STYLE

Developing an effective writing style is a slow process. The more you experiment with the different ways of writing, the more you will become comfortable with certain stylistic techniques that suit you.

For now, though, there are some very basic matters of style that you can master in your writing. You can learn to revise your writing so that it has a consistent point of view, so that it avoids wordiness, and so that it uses precise diction.

Maintaining Consistency in Point of View

One of the obligations that you have as a writer is to maintain a consistency in the point of view from which you develop your subject. _Point of view_ defines the focus from which you "see" or write about your topic. It is important that this point of view be consistent throughout the paragraph or essay; otherwise, you risk jarring your reader's attention from what you are saying to your inconsistency. Sometimes a lack of consistency results in a serious error in usage. At other times, it is simply a matter of style.

There are five basic aspects of consistency with which you should concern yourself. As you will see in the following sections of this unit, you frequently establish your point of view with one of the very first sentences in a piece of writing. This places a further responsibility on you as the writer. You must be unusually careful to phrase that key sentence so it will appropriately establish the point of view that you intend, then you must maintain that point of view consistently throughout the paragraph or essay.

Tense. When you set out to develop a piece of writing, you must determine the time reference for the whole. Is it past? Present? Future? Once that time reference has been established, you should not shift unnecessarily to another form.

The automobile comes slowly down the street. Suddenly it picked up speed and spun around the corner.	**inconsistent**
The automobile comes slowly down the street. Suddenly it picks up speed and spins around the corner.	**consistent**
Team members seem unusually excited, but they didn't know why.	**inconsistent**
Team members seem unusually excited, but they don't know why.	**consistent**

Exercise 2

Rewrite the following short paragraphs so they maintain tense consistency:

1. The story we read that I liked the best was Nathaniel Hawthorne's "Young Goodman Brown." It was a well-written summarization of the hypocrisy of much early American life. Brown's wife is named Faith. Both of them wanted to join a group of witches, but each of them is dishonest with the other.

2. Because his father is a dentist, Joe gets free checkups regularly. He had one of the most handsome smiles around. He told me once that he goes in every three months to get his teeth cleaned.

3. When you called yesterday, I had already done all of my morning chores. I had walk the dogs about 6:30. I also clean the kitchen and made my bed. I was completely ready for the day to begin.

Although the English language recognizes several tenses, you can avoid most tense shifts if you learn to use the following three correctly.

Present

This tense describes an action currently taking place.

I *am* hungry.
You *are* hungry.
Alexandra *is* hungry.

Sometimes the present progressive tense form is also used. This form uses the present tense verb and another, -*ing* verb form:

I *am eating.*
You *are eating.*
Alexandra *is eating.*

Past

This tense describes an action that has already taken place.

I *wrote* you a letter.
You *called* me last Friday.
Jim *answered* the telephone.

The past perfect tense permits you to indicate a time sequence for past actions. It describes an action that was completed before another past action. In the sentence "When you called yesterday, I had already completed all of my morning chores," the verb *called* puts the sentence in the past tense; the use of *had* with *completed* simply indicates that the chores were completed before the call came. The past perfect tense uses a helping verb plus the past participle verb form.

Future

This tense describes an action that will take place at a future time. It is formed by using either *will* or *shall* with the present form of the verb:

I *shall* take the test tomorrow.
You *will* not *forget* to return my book.
Larry probably *will be* late again.

Exercise 3

Examine the following topic sentences, then in the space provided indicate the tense pattern of the proposed paragraph by using the labels *present*, *past*, or *future*.

_____ 1. Because everyone in the family works late, Susan has to cook dinner every night.
_____ 2. Shakespeare used many actual events from history to develop his plays.
_____ 3. I fondly remember the way food smelled at my grandmother's on Thanksgiving Day.
_____ 4. I answered the emergency call, but Jim had arrived and taken care of the crisis before I got there.
_____ 5. We are working extremely hard to get ready for our accounting exam.
_____ 6. My neighbor and I will plant a garden next spring in the plot of land between our houses.
_____ 7. The lake had been polluted long before the new state officials were elected.
_____ 8. The grocery store is always crowded on Saturday, but last week it was more crowded than usual.

Sometimes your topic sentence may indicate two different tense patterns. In these instances, the major time indicators you use in the paragraph will depend upon the manner in which you elect to develop the subject. If your topic sentence states "My vacation was not at all like the one my cousin describes," you might focus on your own vacation (past tense), or you might direct emphasis toward the way your cousin describes (present tense) his or her own vacation.

Just because the topic sentence indicates a specific tense does not mean that you use that tense for every sentence in the paragraph. You change tense, however, only when that change is dictated by the thought process you are developing.

Exercise 4

Below is a paragraph in which the proper form of the verbs has been omitted. Rewrite the paragraph completely three times: once in the *present* tense, once in the *past* tense, and once in the *future* tense.

Working and going to school at the same time _____ (be) challenging for me, but I _____ (know) what to expect well ahead of time. My boss _____ (expect) me to keep working at least twenty-five hours a week, and I _____ (be) in class another twelve hours. Also, I _____ (need) another ten or fifteen hours to study my lessons. I _____ (find) time for this activity early in the mornings before my classes. Later in the day I _____ (slip) in another hour for reading. Doing both things _____ (keep) me busy, but I _____ (enjoy) both my work and my classes. I _____ (give) each of them my best effort.

Number. Nouns and pronouns are either singular or plural in number. You must not change the number when you refer to the same noun or pronoun later in your paragraph or essay.

The problem with consistency of number most often occurs when you are using pronouns. You may carelessly shift from a singular noun such as *person* to a plural pronoun such as *they* later in the sentence or paragraph. Or you may forget which pronouns are singular and which are plural. This problem most often happens with the definite pronouns. The following chart should help.

always singular	always plural	either singular or plural (depending upon sentence pattern)
each	both	most
every	many	some
everyone	several	all
everybody	few	none
nobody		any
either		more
neither		
one		
anyone		
anybody		
someone		
somebody		

You establish the number of a noun or pronoun the first time that you use it in a sentence, and you must not change that number unnecessarily in later references.

A teacher has a responsibility to help students who ask for additional aid outside of class. They must not refuse to provide that assistance. **inconsistent**

A teacher has a responsibility to help students who ask for additional aid outside the class. The teacher must not refuse to provide that assistance. **consistent**

Every one of the students was able to complete their assignment on time. **inconsistent**

Every one of the students was able to complete his or her assignment on time. **consistent**

Exercise 5

In the space provided, label each of these as either *singular* or *plural*.

_____ 1. People reveal a lot about themselves by the way they dress.

_____ 2. Neither of the books was available in the college library.

_____ 3. All of the cake was eaten before I got to the party.

_____ 4. All of the politicians voted along party lines.

_____ 5. Happiness had become a way of life for the two of them.

_____ 6. Nobody bothered to ask for additional assistance with the assignment.

_____ 7. Either of my teachers would have been eager to help.

_____ 8. Both of them are extremely qualified.

_____ 9. Some of the songs that she sang were absolutely horrible.

_____ 10. Some of the music made me extremely angry.

Exercise 6

Rewrite the following short paragraphs so they maintain consistency of number.

1. Everyone called the event a major tragedy. They said that it was something from a nightmare world and that these things must never be allowed to happen again.

2. The basketball team played unusually well last Friday night. For once, it looked worthy of wearing the school colors. They deserved the ovation even though they did not win the game.

3. If anyone calls for me at work tomorrow, tell them that I will return the call promptly. I am expecting some important calls from Mr. Gerhardt, and I do not want to miss them.

4. When you write, your audience has a right to know what it should consider serious and what it should consider humorous. Your writing must make these distinctions clear for them.

5. I read the newspaper articles carefully, but I still do not understand what they were saying. In only one of them did the writer make their opinions vividly precise. Several were extremely vague in what it really wanted to say.

Person. Pronouns are either first person (the person[s] speaking), second person (the person[s] spoken to), or third person (the person[s] or thing[s] spoken about). An unnecessary shift from one person to another can confuse your reader and detract from what you are trying to communicate.

first-person pronouns

singular	plural	
I	we	nominative form
me	us	objective form
my/mine	our/ours	possessive form

second-person pronouns

singular	plural	
you	you	nominative form
you	you	objective form
your/yours	your/yours	possessive form

third-person pronouns

singular	plural	
he, she, it, who, whoever	they, who whoever	nominative form
her, him, it, whom, whomever	them, whom, whomever	objective form
his, her/hers, its, whose	their/theirs, whose	possessive form

A look at this list of forms suggests that the second-person pronoun is the simplest to use, but it is also the one that causes the most trouble in shifts of person.

People who play bridge develop a keen sense of concentration. You simply cannot let your mind wander from the action.

inconsistent

People who play bridge develop a keen sense of concentration. They simply cannot let their minds wander from the action.

consistent

I do not understand why the speaker spoke so softly. You could hardly hear her.

inconsistent

I do not understand why the speaker spoke so softly. I could hardly hear her.

consistent

The easiest shift of person to make, and perhaps the most serious error, is the shift that involves *you*. A careful writer will also avoid shifting to the indefinite pronoun *one* (or its combinations, such as *someone* and *anyone*) when the previous pronoun has been specific.

The movie, even with all of its foreign dialogue, was an experience that I will long remember. One always enjoys something that thoroughly artistic.

inconsistent

The movie, even with all of its foreign dialogue, was an experience that I will long remember. I always enjoy something that thoroughly artistic

consistent

Exercise 7

Rewrite the following short paragraphs so that they maintain consistency of person.

1. If you stay up too late at night, you will not be alert the following morning. One needs six or eight hours sleep to function adequately.

2. Individuals should not be too quick to criticize others. You never know all of the problems they may have had in their lives.

3. Some people think that courage is something that one is born having; others think that it is something you have to develop.

4. Students enrolled in the nursing program have to be especially dedicated. You have to spend long hours in on-the-job training at the hospital.

5. I just don't understand how Bruce could have forgotten the meeting. One should have remembered the time since it was announced every day.

Exercise 8

Completely rewrite the following paragraph three times: once in the first person, once in the second person, and once in the third person.

My favorite summer activity is going to the beach and swimming. When it is 90°, most people think only of finding some way to keep cool and to relax at the same time. Going to the beach is certainly one way that you can do both. One can plunge into the water to keep cool, or you can just lounge along the water's edge to relax. Sometimes people make a complete ritual of going to the beach. You pack a picnic lunch, bring along some drinks and a portable radio. Then one is prepared for a long afternoon of relaxation. If only I did not have to work, I would probably go to the beach every day.

Voice.   When the word *voice* is used to describe an aspect of writing, it refers to the distinction between active and passive. Good writing does not mix these two voices without adequate cause.

Active voice writing requires that the subject perform the action (verb) upon something or someone (the direct object).

Eugene *hurled* the *ball* into the water.
My supervisor *threw* the *report* into the wastebasket.

Active voice is the style of writing generally preferred in written English. It is usually shorter than the passive voice, and it also permits you to have more control over which verb you select and to put that verb in a more dramatic sentence position.

Passive voice writing requires the subject of the verb to receive the action; thus the action passes back to the sentence subject.

The *ball* was *hurled* into the water by Eugene.
The *report* was *thrown* into the wastebasket by my supervisor.

The passive voice always makes use of some form of the verb *to be: is, am, are, was, be, being,* and *been.*

If you begin writing in the active voice, you should maintain that voice throughout your sentence or paragraph. Shifts in voice usually occur between sentence halves or in two sequential sentences that are closely related in subject matter.

The party was planned by Susan, and she in-   **inconsistent**
vited the guests herself.

The party was planned by Susan, and the   **consistent**
guests were invited by her.

Larry wanted to make good grades in his courses at one time. Now, though, that plan has been dropped by him.

inconsistent

Larry wanted to make good grades in his courses at one time. Now, though, he has dropped that plan.

consistent

Rewrite each of the following sequences to maintain consistency of voice.

1. Studying for a test is really easy. First, you should reread all of your class notes. Next, summaries of those notes should be made. Finally, orally review the material until you know it by heart.

2. To prepare for a job interview, you need to anticipate possible questions, prepare tentative responses, and your weakness should then be discussed with a friend or adviser.

3. Luis upholstered the chair himself. The wooden legs were then sanded and painted by him also.

4. The hurricane winds blew the television antenna down, and the windows in the building were also broken.

5. If you are a careful driver, a safe speed is maintained at all times, unusual road conditions are constantly observed, and you obey all traffic laws.

Exercise 10

The following paragraph is written entirely in the passive voice. Rewrite it into the active voice.

The students had really been cheated by the incident. Tickets to the dance were sold by the freshman committee three weeks ahead of time. They were bought very quickly by students who knew the band and admired them. An exciting evening was anticipated by everyone. Thirty tickets were even bought by teachers who wanted to attend. The fraud had not been detected by anyone at that time. Two days before the dance it was discovered by the class president. The news was announced by the Dean of Student Affairs. Students on other campuses had been cheated by this same promoter. The band had been broken up by its organizers two months ago. The money could not be recovered by school officials. Students had been cheated out of their money and a good time.

Tone.   *Tone* refers to the attitude that you as a writer take to both your subject and your audience. Such words as *formal, dignified, serious, humorous, casual, confidential, friendly, satirical, personal,* and *rude* are often used to describe the tone of various pieces of writing.

The tone of your writing may be suggested by the style of your sentences. If your tone is friendly, for instance, you will probably have shorter sentences than you would have in a formal piece of writing. Your tone is suggested by sentences that sound like the casual conversation of two friends.

Your tone is certainly also suggested by the language that you use. In a friendly or casual piece of writing, you will probably use contractions (*can't, don't,* and so forth) instead of the more formal words (*cannot, do not,* etc.). Also, you will probably use words very familiar to your audience, perhaps even some words that hold a special meaning for you and your reader.

As with the other topics discussed in this unit, the tone of a piece of writing is usually suggested by the very first sentence. If you begin writing in a serious, formal tone, do not suddenly shift to a casual, chatty one. If your entire attitude is informal, do not inject formal or ceremonious words into your writing.

The doctor carefully evaluated the medical data and then informed the patient that he was not in danger of croaking.	**inconsistent**
The doctor carefully evaluated the medical data and then informed the patient that he was not in danger of dying.	**consistent**
You can't believe how wild everyone was. They were drinking and generally not giving a damn. Then the supervisor appeared and expressed discountenance.	**inconsistent**
You can't believe how wild everyone was. They were drinking and generally not giving a damn. Then the boss came in and told them off.	**consistent**

Exercise 11

Rewrite the following passages so that they maintain consistency of tone.

1. Those who are called upon to assist in the difficult task of restoring pride and order to our cities must be strong and dedicated individuals. There is no room in this area for individuals with cocky attitudes or for those who wish only to promote their own sidekicks.

2. My friends and I had been ripped off again. When we came home from the midnight show, the first thing we saw was the open window. Then we saw the inside of the room. Man, was it a mess! They took my stereo, cameras, and everything. I just wish the police were more cognizant of what is happening in our neighborhood.

3. Sometimes on Saturday nights all I want to do is get together with the fellows and rap. We throw back some suds and interact together for several hours.

4. The general inefficiency of the tax office has resulted in hundreds of thousands of dollars in lost revenue for the city. Finally the police have busted one clerk for embezzling funds and three more have been fired for their generally creepy attitude.

Exercise 12

Assume that you are going to discuss an issue of current importance with two people. One is your closest friend; the other is someone in authority whom you respect. In the first column below, list words that you will use when you talk with your friend. In the second column list the comparable words that you will use when you talk with the other person.

talking with friend	talking with person in authority
1. _____	1. _____
2. _____	2. _____
3. _____	3. _____
4. _____	4. _____
5. _____	5. _____
6. _____	6. _____
7. _____	7. _____
8. _____	8. _____
9. _____	9. _____
10. _____	10. _____

Exercise 13

For the following series of paragraphs, you will need to recall one of the craziest or wildest parties you ever attended. If you have never been to such a party, use your imagination.

1. Write a one-paragraph description of the party to someone in authority, perhaps the college president or maybe a priest, minister, or rabbi. The individual to whom you write has asked for additional information about the party after hearing that it was unusually rowdy. Use language and selection of details best suited to convince this person of the respectability of the party.

2. Write a one-paragraph description of the party to one of your closest friends who was unable to attend. Your goal this time is to make him or her extremely sorry that he or she missed such a wild, fun-filled event.

3. The audience for your next paragraph description of the party is one of your instructors. You want to impress this person with your sophistication, but you do not want to be offensive or crude.

Avoiding Wordiness

Your first drafts of a piece of writing are often unnecessarily wordy. Some of this wordiness may actually be a form of *redundancy*, saying the same thing twice. Look at these examples:

redundant	concise
advance forward	advance
sit down in a chair	sit in a chair
visible to the eye	visible
dead body	body
at 9 A.M. in the morning	at 9 A.M.

In other instances, your wordiness may simply be the result of your dependence on certain tired expressions that have crept into our language but that are much more effective when reduced to a single word or a shorter phrase:

wordy	concise
in the vicinity of	near
due to the fact that	because
as the sun began to rise	at sunrise
for the purpose of beginning	to begin
at this point in time	now

Here is a short paragraph that has been edited to eliminate wordiness. See how much tighter it is in a revised form.

At 4 o'clock yesterday afternoon a very large group of some accounting majors met with one of the chief accountants of the largest banking firms that exists in our city. He talked orally to us about what we needed to do for the purpose of being successful in our accounting careers. He said that it was his hope that we would blend together our academic studies with the new innovations in technology. The final *by* *urging*

~~conclusion of his comments~~ ~~urged~~ us to ~~settle down to doing some~~ hard

[work] now if we want to be ~~considered a success~~ *successful* in the future.

Exercise 14

Using the work above as a model, edit the following paragraph to cut out unnecessary words and phrases.

I still enjoy hearing my grandfather talk about past history. He always begins telling his stories aloud in a voice filled with a kind of half laugh. And while he talks both of his eyes twinkle due to the fact that he is having so much fun. He is always more than willing to sit up until twelve o'clock midnight talking if someone is there to listen to him. His favorite story took place Easter Sunday in the year 1922. That was the date in time when he proposed marriage to the woman who would become my grandmother. He can tell that story with so many different new twists in reference to their courting days that it sounds like a brand new tale every time I hear it. But what is really fun is when he tells the story and grandmother is nearby in the same room and can hear what he is saying. She keeps correcting everything that she hears him say, and then they get into a mild argument about what really took place at that point in time back in 1922. And in all of these sixty-five years they still can agree among themselves on how things really and truly did happen in 1922.

Using Precise Diction

When you write the first draft, you are intent upon getting your ideas on paper. You write the first words that come to your mind. Those words, though, are not necessarily the most effective ones for you to use. As you revise, you must evaluate each word or set of words carefully to determine if that word or set of words is the best to express your meaning most effectively.

When you write your first draft, you probably have a tendency to use general words, especially nouns, instead of specific ones. As you revise, you must substitute the more specific words. Look at these examples:

general	specific
game	backgammon
car	1968 Chevy
plant	English ivy
building	Rachelle Schmidt Hall
dog	aging dachshund

Now look at the differences between the sentences that use specific as opposed to general diction:

general	specific
No one wanted to play the game with him yesterday.	None of his classmates wanted to play backgammon with him yesterday.
I wouldn't take anything for my car.	I wouldn't take $5,000 for my 1968 Chevy.
He carefully placed a plant on his bookcase.	He carefully placed an English ivy on his bookcase.
I want you to see the lobby of a building with me.	I want you to see the lobby of Rachelle Schmidt Hall with me.
The dog slept in the afternoon sun.	The aging dachshund slept in the afternoon sun.

Exercise 15

Use specific diction to rewrite the following paragraph. Pay attention to the general nouns used in this first draft.

My best friend and I went shopping yesterday afternoon at our favorite store. We actually had some trouble getting there because it was a holiday and the street was so crowded with other shoppers. When we finally got inside, I went directly to the cologne counter to buy some cologne. In addition to the cologne,

I also bought some hair spray and skin toner. My friend wanted to look at the sale on men's clothes. Although he really wanted to buy a designer shirt, he could not afford the price so he settled for a couple of other things instead. After we had spent most of our money, we went to the coffee shop to eat. I ordered a salad and a drink and my friend had soup followed by a huge piece of pie. On the way out of the store, we saw a locally famous football player autographing his book for buyers. But we didn't have the price of the book, so we just watched the people for awhile and then went home.

As you revise, you should become increasingly aware of the differences between the denotative and the connotative meaning of words. The denotative meaning of a word is its dictionary meaning, and all words obviously have denotative (or dictionary) meanings. The connotative meaning of a word is the emotional meaning, and a large number of words have connotative meanings, too. Some connotative words have positive emotional meanings, others negative. Look at these:

denotative	connotative
dog	stray, mutt, mongrel, pooch, puppy, mascot
car	rattle trap, gas eater, wheels, limousine
speak	mutter, stammer, scream, talk, enunciate
walk	hobble, limp, saunter, skip, prance

The more you revise your own work, the more you will learn to let the connotative meaning of words help you to achieve the emotional effect that your writing needs.

Exercise 16

The words in the following paragraph have been purposely chosen to reflect denotative meaning only. Rewrite the paragraph by using positive, connotative diction.

The young boy walked slowly along the shore of the lake with his dog. No one paid any attention to them. The boy was dressed in ordinary clothes, and the dog was of the most common street variety. As they walked along, the boy led his dog by a leash. The heavy wind blew lake water against the shore, and the mist hit both boy and dog, but the boy just bent his head down and kept walking. Finally they got to a very private part of the beach, and the boy took a brown sack from under his coat. He first gave half a sandwich to his dog; then he slowly ate the other half. After their lunch, the two of them went back to the shade of a large rock and fell asleep. I don't think that they ever did know that I had followed them all afternoon and that I sat for another hour watching them sleep. And to this day I can't explain the force that made me give up a whole afternoon to follow that pair along the lake and to their special hideaway.

Exercise 17

Now, rewrite the same paragraph, but using negative diction.

REVISING FOR GRAMMAR AND MECHANICS

Revising your paper for grammar and mechanics is usually the last step in your revision process. As you are rewriting the paper from earlier drafts, you will probably "catch" a few problems and correct them as you go; but your main objective there is to develop your composition in an organized and interesting manner. Once you are satisfied that you have accomplished that task, then you are ready to edit your work for problems with grammar and mechanics.

When you begin editing, be aware of the typical problems that you have with these skills and read your paper with an eye toward editing for those problems. If you know that you frequently have problems with verb tenses, for instance, or that you typically misuse the colon, pay special attention to these two areas as you edit. On the other hand, if you rarely or never have problems with subject–verb agreement or if you always use quotation marks correctly, you need not spend much energy checking in these areas.

Perhaps a checklist like the following will help you as you edit your work the final time:

A Grammar and Mechanics Checklist

- Are the word groups that you have punctuated as sentences, in fact, complete sentences?

- Have you avoided run-on sentences and comma splices?

- Do all of the subjects and verbs agree with each other in number?

- Have you used the correct verb tense and the correct verb form in every instance?

- Have you maintained consistency of verb tense throughout the piece of writing?

- Are your pronouns correct in both number and case?

- Have you maintained consistency of person throughout the piece of writing?

- Have you begun all of your sentences with capital letters and ended them with appropriate end punctuation?

- Have you used internal marks of punctuation correctly?

- Have you checked the words that you are most likely to have misspelled?

As you edit your work for grammar and mechanics, you might read the paper through separately for each of the skills listed above. Later, you will learn to read for several different skills at the same time.

One of the difficulties about this final editing process is that you tend to read what you *think* you have written rather than what you actually have written. For this reason, some experienced editors like to read a piece of writing from the bottom up. If you start with the last sentence of your composition, then move to the next-to-last sentence, and continue reading your essay in reverse, you will force yourself to read individual sentences more carefully and you will not get lost so readily in the ideas.

THE GENESIS OF AN ESSAY

On the following pages you have the rough draft, two revisions, and a final essay prepared by Carolynn Monroe. If you study the changes that Carolynn made in the various stages of her project, you will begin to understand how you might improve your own work through revision.

Rough Draft

"Over the river & through the woods to Grandmother's house we go" (etc.) (etc.) is a happy song, but brings sadness to my heart. I remember packing up the baby (parafanelia), ~~making sure~~ feeling a bit like Santa making a list & checking *it* twice & hoping I didn't forget anything. Grandma didn't live in Timbuktu, but the long hot drive ~~was~~ *seemed* half way around the world. Chug, chugging along on the expressway for an hr & a half, grateful my car had air cond. I wondered what this trip would be like if these were the horse & buggy days. I'd be trudging along a cracked, dry, dirt road, eating ~~flying~~ dust & ~~horse~~ smelling horse tails. The sound of a car horn & a big grn street sign ahead, brings me out of my daydream & back to reality, I have arrived at G's street. Driving down her block, I muster up the courage & cheerfulness needed for the rest of my journey. Climbing 2 flights of stairs, my legs felt like I was wearing iron combat boots. Entering Grandma's apt, I was almost blinded by sun reflection of the ~~sun~~ on the light colored linoleum flopr. The little speckles jumped around like twinkling stars. ~~Closing my eyes I get~~...The apt. appeared so clean, so bare. It was stripped of the happy sounds, the smell of cooking & the arms of Grandma around me. Grandma used to give the original "bear hugs." I remember getting lost into her skin, like some giant marshmellow was swallowing me. The smell of cooking was replaced by the pungent odor of alcohol. ~~Around the~~ moving further into the apt. & going down the hall I can see Grandma's dresser. Pill bottles stand silently like plastic solders keeping a watchful vigil. Gone are the cologne bottles & pictures of smiling people. Someone is lying in Grandma's bed. She's small, & thin ~~fragile~~ & looks as fragile as a dried old twig. I am afraid if I breath too hard & hug too tight, I might break her like a wishbone. As I lay the baby on the bed for Grandma to touch, I wondered about the times she must have touched her children. Did Grandma ever think about life's cycles? Did she ever wonder if someday her children would be caring for her as she did for them? My aunt walks into the room & smiles warmly, I can't help but think that she is wearing a mask that hides her sadness. "Thank you for coming again," she says. "It is so good to see you both." The small talk continues & then it's time for our goodbyes. I know I'll be back next week, hating every minutes of the journey. It is sad to think that reality cannot be more like a verse of a happy song.

When she wrote this rough draft, Carolynn was primarily concerned with getting her ideas down in some sort of chronological order. Although she did cross out and make a few hurried changes even in this draft, she abbreviated several words as she wrote and even misspelled two. The major grammar problem in this draft is with verb tenses; Carolynn shifts back and forth from past to present. But that problem is not an issue right now; she can correct it as she revises her paper.

First Revision

Here is the work Carolynn did when she revised her paper for the first time. You can see that most of her efforts in this revision were to add details to what she had already written.

Life is not a song, reality is not a verse, and the journey to Grandmother's house isn't always so much fun

"Over the river & through the woods to Grandmother's house we go" etc, etc, is a happy ~~song,~~ *Catchy tune* ~~but~~ brings sadness to my heart. I remember packing up the baby parafanelia, *that paraphernalia* feeling a bit like Santa making a list & checking twice and hoping I didn't forget anything.

Grandma didn't live in Timbuktu, but the long hot drive was half way around the world. Chug, chugging along on the expressway for an hour and a half, *praying that the cars* ~~grateful my car had~~ *would not break down,* air conditioning, I wondered what this trip would be like if these were the horse & buggy days. I'd be ~~trudging~~ *jerking* along a *bumpy* cracked, dry, dirt road, eating flying dust & horse smelling horse tails.

Suddenly, The sound of a car horn ~~and a big grn street sign ahead,~~ brings me out of my daydream and back to reality. ~~I have arrived at G's street.~~ *Ahead, a big green street sign lists Grandma's street.* Driving down her block, I muster up the courage and cheerfulness needed for the rest of my journey. *Taking a big breath, I leave the shelter of the car and* Climb~~ing~~ up two flights of stairs. My legs felt like I *with baby and baggage in hand* was wearing iron combat boots. Entering Grandma's *kitchen* apartment, I was almost blinded by ~~sun's~~ *speckled,* reflection of the sun on the light colored linoleum floor. The little speckles ^(seemed to) jumped around like twinkling stars.

The house appeared so clean, so bare, ^(so quiet.) It was stripped of the happy

sounds, the smell of cooking and the arms of Grandma around me.

Grandma used to give the original "bear hugs." I remember getting lost

into her skin, like ^(I was being) some giant marshmallow. ~~was swallowing me.~~ The

smell of cooking was replaced by the pungent odor of ^(rubbing) alcohol. Moving

further into the kitchen and going down the hall, I could see Grandma's

dresser. Pill bottles ~~stand~~ ^(stood) silently like plastic soldiers keeping a watchful

vigil, ~~Gone are the~~ ^(occupying the place where) cologne bottles and pictures of smiling people ^(used to be.)

Someone is lying in Grandma's bed, ^(I thought.) She's small, and thin and looks as

fragile as a dried old twig. I am afraid if I breath too hard & hug too

tight, I might break her like a wishbone. As I lay the baby on the bed for

Grandma to touch, I wondered about the times she must have touched

Like a song that has a happy little refrain repeated

her children. Did Grandma ever think about life's cycles? Did she ever ^(after every verse)

wonder if someday her children would be caring for her as she did for ^(over and over.)

them? My aunt walks into the room and & smiles warmly. I can't help but ^(again.)

think ~~that~~ she is wearing a mask that hides her ^(sorrow) ~~sadness~~. "Thank you for

coming ~~again~~," she says. "It is so good to see you both." The small talk

continues & then it's time for our goodbyes. I know I'll be back next

week, hating every minutes of the ^(long, tedious) journey, It makes me sad to think that

reluctant to climb on the stairs and enter that

reality cannot be more like a verse of a happy song. ^(medicinal and) (unfamiliar world.)

I see myself as the refrain of a song, coming back over and over again and wishing this could be a happy catchy tune instead of a sad piece of reality.

Second Revision

When Carolynn revised her paper the next time, she continued to add a few more details; but she also edited her grammar and, in some places, made herself notes to check specific sentences before she wrote them into final form.

"Over the river and through the woods to Grandmother's house we

go" ~~etc, etc,~~ is a happy catchy song, that brings sadness to my heart.

Life is not a song, reality is not a verse, and the journey to Grandma's

and his bottles, food, dishes, extra clothes, and toys
house isn't always so much fun. I remember packing up the baby ∧

and
~~paraphernalia~~ feeling a bit like Santa making a list ∧ checking twice ∧and

hoping I didn't forget anything. Grandma didn't live in Timbuktu, but the

long hot drive was half way around the world. Chug, chugging along on

the expressway for an hour and a half, praying that the car's air

contioning would not break down. I wondered what this trip would be

like if these were the horse & buggy days. I'd be jerking along a bumpy,

dry and cracked, dirt road, eating flying dust and smelling horse tails.

Instead, I was,   *jolted*
Suddenly, the sound of a car horn ~~jolts~~ me out of my dream and back to

listed
reality. Ahead a big green street sign ~~lits~~ Grandma's street. Driving down

mustered
her block, I ~~muster~~ up the courage and cheerfulness needed for the rest

left
of my journey. Taking a big breath, I ~~leave~~ the shelter of the car, and with

baby and baggage in hand, I climbed up two flights of stairs. My legs felt

like I was wearing iron combat boots. Entering Grandma's kitchen, I was

almost blinded by the reflection of sun on the speckled, light colored

linoleum. The little speckles seemed to jump around like twinkling stars.

The house appeared so clean, so bare, so quiet. It was stripped of happy sounds, the smell of cooking and the arms of Grandma around me.

work on this sentence

Grandma used to give the original "bear hugs." I remember getting lost into her skin, like I was being swallowed by some some giant

rubbing

marshmallow. The smell of cooking was replaced by the pungent odor of alcohol. Moving further into the kitchen and going down the hall, I could

see Grandma's dresser. Pill bottles stood silently like plastic soldiers

Turning into the room, I noticed

keeping a watchful vigil, occupying the place where cologne bottles and pictures of smiling people used to be. Someone is lying in Grandma's

How Garndma has changed.

bed, I thought. She's small, and thin and looks as fragile as a dried old

Breathed   and   hugged

twig. I am afraid if I ~~breath~~ too hard ~~& hug~~ too tight, I might break her

like a wishbone. As I laid the baby on the bed for Grandma to touch, I

wondered about the times she must have touched her children. Did

Grandma ever think about life's cycles? Like a song that has a happy

little refrain repeated after every verse over and over again. Did she ever

do as one sentence

wonder if someday her children would be caring for her as she did for

walked   smiled

them? My aunt ~~walks~~ into the room and and ~~smiles~~ warmly. I can't help

was   hid

but think she ~~is~~ wearing a mask that ~~hides~~ her sorrow. "Thank you for

said

coming," she ~~says~~. "It is so good to see you both." The small talk

d   was   Knew would

continue~~s~~ and then it ~~is~~ time for our goodbyes. I ~~knew~~ I'll be back next

week, hating every minute~~s~~ of the journey, reluctant to climb the stairs

saw

and enter that medicinal and unfamiliar world. I ~~see~~ myself as the refrain

of a song, coming back over and over again and wishing this would be a

happy, catchy tune instead of a sad piece of reality.

Final Revision

Here is the final version of Carolynn's paper, the one that she submitted to her instructor for a grade. Notice how much it has changed from the original draft.

"Over the river and through the woods to Grandmother's house we go" is a happy, catchy song, that brings sadness to my heart. Life is not a song, reality is not a verse, and the journey to Grandma's house isn't always so much fun. I remember packing up the baby and his bottles, food, dishes, extra clothes, and toys—feeling a bit like Santa making a list and checking it twice—and hoping I didn't forget anything. Grandma didn't live in Timbuktu, but the long, hot drive seemed half-way around the world. I wondered what this trip would be like if these were the horse and buggy days. I'd be jerking along a bumpy, dry, and cracked dirt road, eating dust and smelling horse tails. Instead I was chug, chugging along on the expressway for an hour and a half, praying that the car's air conditioning would not break down. Suddenly, the sound of a car horn jolted me out of my dream and back to reality. Ahead a big green street sign listed Grandma's street. Driving down her block, I mustered up the courage and cheerfulness needed for the rest of my journey. Taking a big breath, I left the shelter of the car, and with baby and baggage in hand, I climbed up two flights of stairs. My legs felt like I was wearing iron combat boots. Entering Grandma's kitchen, I was almost blinded by the reflection of the sun on the speckled, light colored linoleum. The little speckles seemed to jump around like twinkling stars. The house appeared so clean, so bare, so quiet. It was stripped of the happy sounds, the smell of cooking and the arms of Grandma, who used to give the original "bear hugs," around me. I remember getting lost in her skin, like I was being swallowed by some some giant marshmallow. The smell of cooking was replaced by the pungent odor of rubbing alcohol. Moving further into the kitchen and going down the hall, I could see Grandma's dresser. Pill bottles stood silently like plastic soldiers keeping a watchful vigil, occupying the place where cologne bottles and pictures of smiling people used to be. Turning into the room, I noticed someone lying in Grandma's bed, I thought. She's small and thin and looks as fragile as a dried twig. How Grandma has changed. I was afraid if I breathed too hard and hugged too tightly, I might break her like a wishbone. As I laid the baby on the bed for Grandma to touch, I wondered about the times she must have touched her children. Did Grandma ever think about life's cycles—like a song that has a happy little refrain repeated after every verse over and over again—did she ever wonder if someday her children would be caring for her as she did for them? My aunt walked into the room and smiled warmly. I couldn't help but think she was wearing a mask to hide her sorrow. "Thank you for coming," she said. "It is so good to see you both." The small talk continued and then it was time for our goodbye's. I knew I would be back next week, hating every minute of the journey, reluctant to climb the stairs and enter that medicinal and unfamiliar world. I saw myself as the refrain of a song, coming back over and over again and wishing this would be a happy, catchy tune instead of a sad piece of reality.

The Paragraph

The Basics of the Paragraph

Patterns for Organization

Types of Development

C H A P T E R

4

The Basics of the Paragraph

The *paragraph* is often regarded as the basic unit of composition. An individual sentence is too short to develop any involved thought pattern, but a set of closely related sentences can develop such a pattern. Without realizing the formal structure, most persons think in paragraphlike units most of the time. Reflect upon your own daydreaming patterns. You think about last night's date for a few minutes; you skip to that long assignment that you must prepare for tomorrow's chemistry class; then you remember that you have to stop to pick up the cleaning on your way home. In each of these idea groupings, your mind wanders through more than one sentence. In each of the three groupings, you collect related ideas and hold them together until you are ready to move on to another set of ideas.

A paragraph is just that—a set of related sentences held together by structural and contextual unity. That is, the sentences in a paragraph are purposely designed to fit together, and the ideas being developed in the paragraph further help to bind the material together.

Learning how to write effective paragraphs is an important step toward learning how to write effective essays. In many ways, the paragraph is a kind of mini-essay. If you are able to master the skills necessary to write a good paragraph, you should have little difficulty in writing an essay, which is, after all, just a series of closely connected paragraphs.

INDENTATION

Writers typically indent the first word of each new paragraph to let their readers know that they are beginning a new idea or moving to another section of the development of their original idea.

Indenting a paragraph is like punctuating a sentence; indeed, indentation is a form of punctuation. You signal the beginning of every new paragraph by indenting the first word. Although style manuals vary, the most generally accepted indentation for a typed manuscript is five spaces. In a handwritten manuscript, indent approximately one half inch. The actual amount of space you indent doesn't matter as much as the consistency with which you use it. Settle on a definite amount of space for indentation and use it for *all* of your paragraph indentations. Also, remember to fill out your lines. Do not stop short of your right-hand margin until the very last word of your paragraph.

Your objective as a writer is to communicate with your reader. Since most readers have come to regard indentation as a formal signal of a paragraph—one of the accepted conventions of the writer–reader relationship—you should present your paragraphs as your reader expects them, properly indented with lines properly filled out to both left and right margins. Look at these examples:

Correct Indentation and Margins

       Learning how to write effective paragraphs is an important step toward learning how to write effective essays. In many ways, the paragraph is a kind of mini-essay. If you are able to master the skills necessary to write a good paragraph, you should have little difficulty in writing an essay, which is, after all, just a series of closely connected paragraphs.

Incorrect Indentation and Faulty Right Margins

Learning how to write effective paragraphs is an important step toward learning how to write effective essays. In many ways, the paragraph is a kind of mini-essay. If you are able to master the skills necessary to write a good paragraph, you should have little difficulty in writing an essay, which is, after all, just a series of closely connected paragraphs.

Incorrect Indentation and Faulty Left Margins

Learning how to write effective paragraphs is an important step toward learning how to write effective essays. In many ways, the paragraph is a kind of mini-essay. If you are able to master the skills necessary to write a good paragraph, you should have little difficulty in writing an essay, which is, after all, just a series of closely connected paragraphs.

Normally the paragraph requires no more marking than it receives from being indented. However, certain forms of writing often have extra spacing between paragraphs so that their individual ideas can stand out even more easily. For example, when typing business letters, writers always type each paragraph single-spaced and double-space between the individual paragaphs. Sometimes your English instructor may ask you to double-space between your paragraphs when you write them single-spaced. Such a technique makes it easier to see the paragraph as a separate unit.

TOPIC SENTENCES

A paragraph is a set of sentences about a limited topic. As a writer, you should provide your reader with as much help as possible to understand your ideas. One proven method for providing this help is to give each paragraph focus through a *topic sentence*. This sentence announces the topic of the paragraph in a very specific manner.

The topic sentence is generally found at the beginning of a paragraph, even of paragraphs written by highly skilled professional writers. However, the more skilled a writer is, the more he or she is able to experiment with placement of the topic sentence. Sometimes the topic sentence is at the beginning of a paragraph, sometimes in the middle of the paragraph, and sometimes at the end of the paragraph. Occasionally, a paragraph has only an implied topic sentence.

The main requirement of a good topic sentence is that it clearly announce the subject matter of the paragraph. Since a paragraph is usually no more than eight or ten sentences long, it cannot develop a lengthy or highly complex idea. One weakness of many topic sentences is that they offer to cover too much territory.

1. We need to save more of our natural resources.
2. Racism is still active in America.   **weak**
3. Vacations are terribly exciting.   **topic**
4. Returning to school has changed my life.   **sentences**
5. A lot of people cheat on their income-tax forms.

Although each of these sentences does present a topic, each is weak because the topic is either vague (What natural resources? What kind of racism? What is meant by exciting?) or too broad (How many people? What types of cheating?).

You should design a topic sentence to be as specific as possible. One way to do this is to apply the general questions journalists ask—*who, what, when, where, why,* and *how*—to vague or broad statements. Just by answering one or two of these questions, you will limit your topic and give it a much more specific focus.

1. We can conserve our natural resources by follow-ing three simple rules.   (*how*)
   We need to conserve our natural resources by driving less.   (*how*)
   We need to save more of our oil re-serves.   (*what*)
2. Racism is still active in the office where I work.   (*where*)   **improved**
   Racial strife at Ogden High School has affected   **topic**
   both white and black students.   (*where, who*)   **sentences**
3. Vacations in Spain are terribly exciting.   (*where*)
   Vacations provide a change of scenery and a chance to relax without worrying about work-related problems.   (*what, how*)
4. Beginning my nursing program at Fratt Commu-nity College has changed my life.   (*what, where*)
   Returning to school at the age of forty-three, I

now find a variety of career opportunities available to me.   (*when, what*)

My Uncle Frank cheats on his income-tax forms.   (*who*)

A large number of people cheat on their income-tax forms by claiming excessive travel deductions.   (*how*)

improved topic sentences

Answering the questions *who, what, when, where, why,* and *how* can sometimes give you a variety of ways to look at the same topic (a kind of brainstorming) to see what aspect about it most interests you. Look at the following example:

broad topic	questions	limited topics
clothes	who	Allen wears the craziest combination of clothes that I have ever seen.
	what	Punk clothes have certainly replaced the preppy look on my campus.
	when	Dressing up in my best clothes is one way that I have of making myself feel better on depressing days.
	where	I thought I had seen every possible kind of bathing suit, but that was before I went to Hawaii last summer.
	why	After everybody laughed at my tennis outfit, I guess I will have to get rid of it and buy a new one.
	how	I don't like shopping for clothes, so I just sit down and order everything from a catalog.

Exercise 1

Select one of the broad topics below and write your own topic sentences by asking the six journalistic questions.

Broad topics: friends, neighborhoods, sports, jobs

limited topics

1. (who) _____

_____

2. (what) _____

_____

3. (when) _____

_____

4. (where) _____

_____

5. (why) _____

_____

6. (how) _____

_____

Exercise 2

Here are fifteen sentences. Some of them are good topic sentences; others are too broad to handle within the 100 or so words of a typical paragraph. Place a check beside those that are narrow enough as they now stand. Explain which journalistic questions are answered.

_____ **1.** I do not particularly like studying for my accounting class.

_____ **2.** Politics and politicians are both evil.

_____ **3.** Football is an exciting sport.

_____ **4.** Different kinds of food interest different people.

_____ **5.** My sister and her husband are seeing a marriage counselor.

_____ **6.** Winter is very depressing.

_____ **7.** Ms. Schwartz is my best teacher.

_____ **8.** Opera is an exciting art form for me.

_____ **9.** Using a dictionary is helpful.

_____ **10.** Going to school and working at the same time is very difficult.

_____ **11.** Christmas is too commercial.

_____ **12.** Too many federal laws are unnecessary.

_____ **13.** Registration for college is confusing.

_____ **14.** I have a difficult time living within my budget.

_____ **15.** Education is very advantageous.

Exercise 3

Although all of the sentences in the exercise could be made even more specific, nine of them are so vague or broad that you could not use them to develop good paragraphs. Rewrite five of those sentences below, making each of them more specific or more limited. Use one or two of the journalistic questions—who, what, when, where, why, and how—with each sentence to help provide focus.

Example: Winter is very drepressing because I have to spend too much of my time cooped up inside my house. (answers the _why_ questions)

1. _____

_____

2. _____

_____

3. _____

_____

4. _____

_____

5. _____

_____

Exercise 4

Select one of these topic sentences and develop it into a short paragraph by adding five or six supporting sentences of your own.

UNITY

A paragraph exists to develop an idea. It is important that each paragraph develop one specific idea and no more. If a paragraph develops more than one idea, it fails to have *unity*. If it does not develop an idea at all, it does not fulfill its function.

Every paragraph should have a reason for existing. No paragraph should be in a composition just because the writer thought it was time to indent again. A good writer is always able to give a specific reason for each paragraph in his or her composition.

Too often a writer is tempted to gather random thoughts into several sentences, indent them, and call them a paragraph. Look at the following example. It begins nowhere and goes nowhere. It has no purpose.

I feel quite confident about the math test that is scheduled for tomorrow. The instructor has told us exactly what to study, and my grades on homework have been good. After the test, Susan and I are going to eat and then go to a movie. She is taking me out because it is my birthday. Last week we were going to go to the homecoming game, but she was sick and we didn't get to go.

The paragraph has no unity because it has no single topic. The writer discusses three different things: the math test, his upcoming date with Susan, and the missed date last week. Each of these topics might be developed into a paragraph or even a complete essay, but all three certainly do not belong together in one paragraph.

The topic sentence is the major unifying force within your paragraph. Every sentence in the paragraph must support the topic sentence. If a sentence in the body of the paragraph does not have a direct relationship with the topic sentence, that sentence does not belong because it violates paragraph unity. In a well-constructed paragraph, the sentences lend support in the following manner:

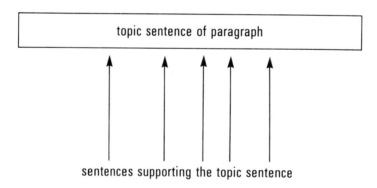

The structure of the student paragraph about the math test looks like this:

> *I feel quite confident about the math test that is scheduled for tomorrow.*

> *The instructor has told us exactly what to study, and my grades on homework have been good.*

> *After the test, Susan and I are going to eat and then go to a movie.*

> *She is taking me out because it is my birthday.*

> *Last week we were going to go to the homecoming game, but she was sick and we didn't get to go.*

Notice that only one sentence can be linked directly back to the topic sentence; that is, only one sentence really offers some development of what should be the main idea of the paragraph.

The student who wrote this paragraph rewrote it into the following unified version.

> I feel quite confident about the math test that is scheduled for tomorrow. The instructor has told us exactly what to study, and my grades on homework have been good. In fact, I suppose that math has always been one of the subjects that I enjoy the most. I have already spent two hours reviewing pages 115–140. Tonight Susan and I will devote another hour or two to practicing with some of the sample problems. Then I will be ready.

Unlike the first effort, this paragraph is now unified because each of the five sentences can be directly linked with the topic sentence, as is obvious in the diagram below.

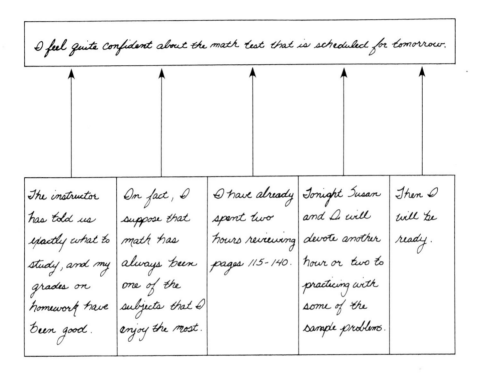

I feel quite confident about the math test that is scheduled for tomorrow.

| The instructor has told us exactly what to study, and my grades on homework have been good. | In fact, I suppose that math has always been one of the subjects that I enjoy the most. | I have already spent two hours reviewing pages 115-140. | Tonight Susan and I will devote another hour or two to practicing with some of the sample problems. | Then I will be ready. |

The topic sentence in this sample paragraph is the very first sentence. As we have said, in more instances than not you will find that the topic sentence is in the introductory position. The more skilled you become as a writer, the more you may experiment with varying the placement of the topic sentence. But even if it is in the middle of the paragraph or at the end, the topic sentence is always the sentence around which all other sentences must be unified.

Each of the following paragraphs contains sentences that support the topic sentence and thus violate paragraph unity. Cross out the sentences that don't belong and then recopy only the remaining sentences.

A. When it is 90°, most people think of finding some way to keep cool and to relax at the same time. Going to the beach is certainly one way to do both. It is only nine blocks from my house. One can plunge into the water to keep cool, or just lounge along the water's edge to relax. My cousin is a lifeguard and is at the beach seven hours every day. He received his training last summer in a special Red Cross program at the YMCA pool. Sometimes people make a complete ritual of going to the beach. They pack a picnic lunch, bring along some drinks and a portable radio. My radio broke last week, but I am going to have it repaired. Some people would be at the beach every day if they did not have to work.

B. I ate at Mama Francine's last night, but the experience was so bad that I will never go back. My date and I had to wait nearly an hour for a table. Sue looked pretty in her new clothes. Finally we were seated at a very small table near the kitchen. I actually think it was a service table for the waiters to use and not one for customers. After we ordered, we sat for another thirty minutes before our salad was brought to the table. I always like salad, especially when it is topped with a good blue-cheese dressing. When the waiter poured our wine, he spilled some of it in Sue's salad plate, and he never offered to clean the mess that he made. There was still a possibility that the main course would redeem everything else. Alas, it was a disappointment too. My veal was dry and stringy. Aunt Helen knows how to cook veal just the way I like it. Sue's steak was so fatty that she didn't even try to eat it. Everything added up to a wasted two hours and a wasted twenty dollars.

C. My father thinks that I am not serious enough about my studies. He says that when he went to college he didn't have time to spend three hours a day listening to music and talking to friends. He works now as an accountant, but he used to work as manager of a dry-cleaning firm. Last night he complained that I had made a C on my math test. I'm just not very good at math, and I know it. He said that if I had studied instead of playing so much I would have done better. When he was a student, all he ever did was study and work. While he was going to college, he worked as a clerk at a neighborhood grocery store. He told me he made seventy-five cents an hour. This morning he became quite angry when I talked to Maurice for an hour on the telephone. He said that such activities as that were what caused me to get bad grades. I guess I really don't think that a C is so terribly bad. Since he pays my bills, I suppose that I will have to try to spend less time listening to music and talking to friends and more time studying.

Controlling Idea

One method for checking to see that your paragraph is unified is to determine how closely each sentence supports your *controlling idea*. The controlling idea is usually indicated by a single word or sometimes a phrase in the topic sentence. Everything in the paragraph must relate to this idea. In the sample paragraph on page 71, the controlling word is *confident*. All details are presented to support the student's confidence.

The following sentences could be topic sentences for paragraphs. Notice the italicized controlling word or phrase.

Mr. Random is a very *stubborn* person.
Mrs. Wilson's *constant generosity* won her the affection of her neighbors.
The excessive heat made any outside activity *unbearable*.
I enjoy my work because of the *convenient schedule* I was given.
My cousin got fired from his job because he was *lazy*.

It is important for you to recognize that the controlling word or idea may not be the same as what appears to be the broad paragraph topic. Rather, it is a limiting or controlled way of looking at that topic.

With certain topic sentences, you might readily shift the control from one place in the sentence to another. Look at these examples:

My old car *broke down* on the busy highway.
My old car broke down on the *busy highway*.
My *old car* broke down on the busy highway.

If you developed this paragraph with a focus on *broke down*, you would use details that explained exactly what happened to your car. If you elected to focus on *busy highway*, you would use details that explained your problems in getting your car to the side of the road without being hit by the rapidly moving traffic. If you focused on *old car*, you would emphasize how old and worn out your car was. The point is that you as the writer must decide what the limited focus of your paragraph will be and write to support that focus.

Exercise 6

Underline the control word in each of the following sentences.

1. Sue Ellen has the weirdest laugh I have ever heard.
2. Ms. Ramirez is the most demanding teacher on this campus.
3. My current job is the easiest one I have ever had.
4. Harry's car is the best kept one in our neighborhood.
5. Eating at that restaurant was a horrible experience.
6. My dog is furiously jealous of my sister's new cat.
7. The new neighbors next door are extremely noisy.
8. Water skiing is my favorite sport.
9. The best vacation I ever had was when I went backpacking alone last summer.
10. Although Robert is the oldest child in my family, he sometimes acts extremely immature.

Exercise 7

Write a topic sentence with a control word or phrase for each of the broad topics listed below. Underline your control word or phrase.

1. a musical group _____

_____

2. a television show _____

_____

3. one of your teachers _____

_____

4. a neighborhood fast-food restaurant _____

_____

5. a local sports team _____

_____

Exercise 8

Select one of these topic sentences and develop it into a short paragraph by adding five or six supporting sentences of your own.

STRUCTURE

You should present the ideas within your paragraph in an organized, systematic manner so that your reader will know the way you are thinking about them. Although an experienced writer may be able to structure ideas almost automatically as he or she writes, you might be better off at the beginning to keep in mind specific structural models that will assist you.

Throughout this text, you will find examples of what are frequently called *fencepost outlines*. These are not outlines in the traditional sense at all, but they are quick schemes for letting you visualize the structure of your paragraph(s).

In the simplest structure for a paragraph, you can quickly make a sketch to show how each of your main supporting ideas relates directly to the topic sentence. A paragraph written from such a scheme would have the topic sentence and one sentence (called a major support sentence) for each of the supporting ideas. Here is a basic format for such a structure:

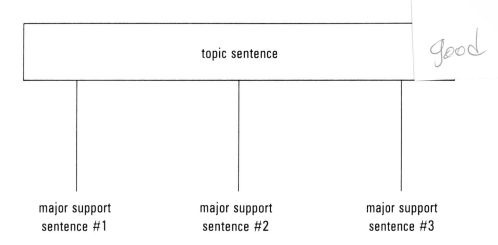

good

Most paragraphs have major supporting sentences that are themselves followed by specific details. These detail sentences further explain ideas suggested by the major supporting sentences. Here is the basic scheme for such a structure:

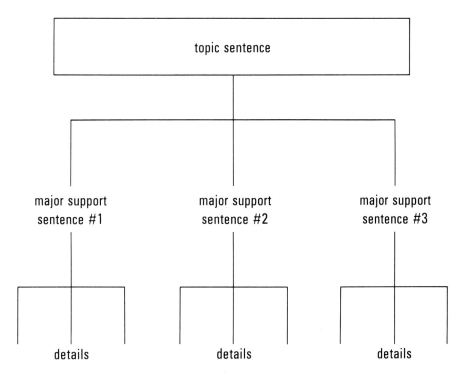

When you are using the fencepost outline to help structure your paragraph, it is not necessary to write complete sentences for every entry. Treat it as you would an ordinary topic outline, simply listing words or phrases to help you visualize the structure of your paragraph. Here is a completed fencepost outline that one student wrote for a paragraph on why he wanted his own apartment:

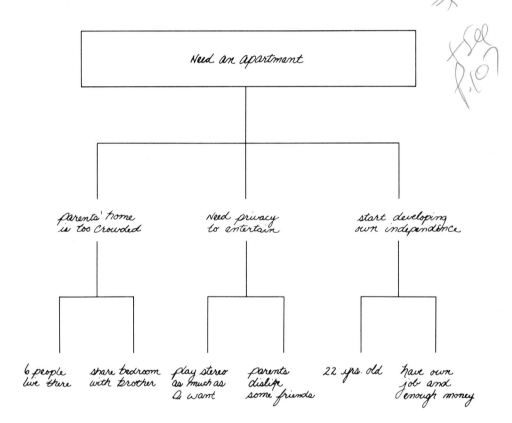

Since most writing becomes interesting when it is developed with sufficient details, it is important that you learn how to arrange minor support ideas to enhance your own style.

Examine this paragraph, which contains a topic sentence followed by three major support statements:

I dislike those types of movies that do not deal with current, real-life situations. Science fiction motion pictures are probably the ones

I dislike the most. Running a close second on my "dislike list" are historic epics. Sentimental love stories represent the third category of movies that I usually try to avoid.

Although there is nothing wrong with this paragraph, it is not especially interesting or informative. You do not know why the writer dislikes these three types of movies, nor do you know which specific movies are on the "dislike list." The writer in this case elected to expand the paragraph by using details in each category to explain why he disliked it.

I dislike those types of movies that do not deal with current, real-life situations. Science fiction	**topic sentence**
motion pictures are probably the ones I dislike the	**major support**
most. Movies with wildly conceived people, animals, or settings from some imaginary world turn me off.	**details**
I would much rather see a scene set in Chicago or New York than in some unreal Planet X. And I prefer real human beings to robots and talking computers. Running a close second on my "dislike	
list" are historic epics. Maybe I don't have enough	**major support**
background, but I find the retelling of past events	**details**
boring. I have enough problems today without worrying about what happened in historic Greece or fifteenth-century England. Sentimental love stories	
represent the third category of movies that I usually	**major support**
try to avoid. In real life everyone does not always	
get his woman or her man. Pretending that love is	**details**
all pleasure and no pain sets up false standards for young people who have to live with real mates. I	
guess I am just a hardheaded realist.	**conclusion**

This paragraph now has some flesh on its structural skeleton. It offers some specific details that give the reader an insight into the writer's thinking. Of course, it could be expanded even more. It would be a simple task for this writer to add another level of supporting details, which in this case would probably include references to specific movies that he dislikes.

When you first begin to think about how you will support a topic sentence, you probably think first of the major points that you wish to make. Whether you write them out formally or simply think them through carefully, you begin at this point to organize your paragraph. Identifying your major support sentences lets you check on the thoroughness of your support and gives you the opportunity to arrange information in its most logical sequence.

After you have thought through the major support points that you want to make, you can then readily add sentences of detail (minor support) where they are needed. Remember that major support sentences relate directly to the topic sentences and detail sentences relate directly to major support sentences.

Exercise 9

Look again at the first example that you had of a unified paragraph (page 71). This paragraph is composed of a topic sentence and a series of major support statements. Below are details. Pry the paragraph apart and insert these statements where they are structurally needed.

He said the test will cover only the work we have done in the last three weeks.

In high school I studied math for three years and made all A's.

I made an A on our first test and A's or B's on every assignment that we have done.

There are three sequences on page 133 that I especially want to study again.

COHERENCE

In addition to unity, a good paragraph must have *coherence*. When things cohere, they stick together. Therefore, the parts of your paragraph must stick together to form a whole. An additional requirement of paragraph coherence is that the parts stick together in a logical relationship. That is, you must use language and structure that will help the reader see the relationship among the several parts of your paragraph.

One important technique for achieving adequate paragraph coherence is to work with *repetition* of words, phrases, or ideas from the topic sentence through the paragraph body. For example, take the topic sentence "I object to censorship for three specific reasons." This sentence indicates that the paragraph will have three parts corresponding to the three reasons for disliking censorship. In this type of development, called development by enumeration, you must be careful to show your movement from one major level of support to the next. You might do this with transition words such as *first, second, third,* or *one reason, another reason, a final reason.*

Although development by enumeration is certainly correct, you do not want to organize all of your paragraphs this way. Another technique is purposely to introduce in the topic sentence a word or phrase that can later serve as a transition marker to separate paragraph parts. Such *transition signals* tell your reader that you are moving to another phrase of the paragraph's development.

There are two basic types of transition signals that you may use to achieve coherence through structural repetition: (1) *repetition by exact word,* in which you repeat the exact word from your topic sentence; and (2) *repetition by synonym,* in which you use another word or phrase suggested by your topic sentence. You will usually use these kinds of transition signals to show movement from one *major* section of your paragraph to another. These sections are those assigned at the major level of support. The following fencepost outline shows the parts of the paragraph that you must carefully tie together to develop proper coherence:

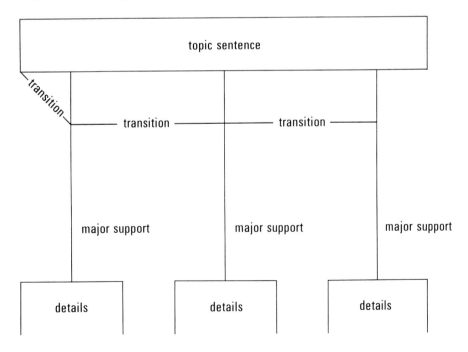

The paragraph below is structured by enumeration. The structural parts are numbered and are anchored back to a listing in the topic sentence of how many parts the paragraph will contain. See how this fencepost outline is developed into a complete paragraph on pages 84–85.

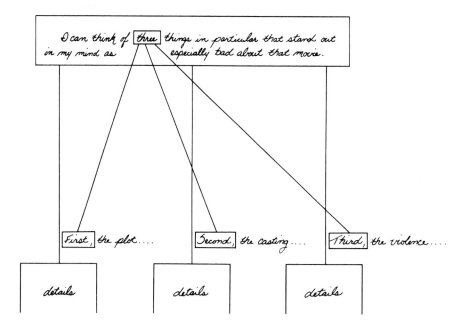

Transition signals become almost automatic with certain types of paragraphs. The example at the top of the next page is typical. In this example, the repetition of the two key words from the topic sentence clearly indicates the two structural parts of the paragraph.

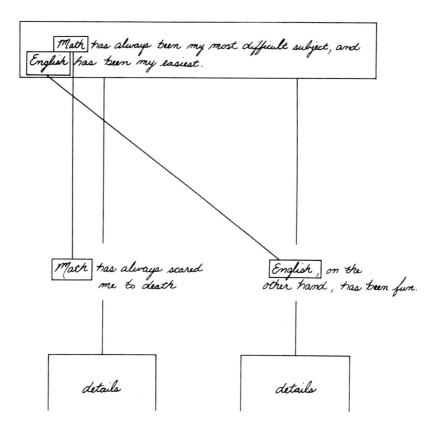

Math has always been my most difficult subject, and English has been my easiest.

Math has always scared me to death

English, on the other hand, has been fun.

details

details

Although you may wish to repeat your control word or phrase once or twice in your paragraph, you do not want to repeat it so often that it makes your writing boring. Learn to use synonyms as a type of repetition. The example at the top of the next page makes effective use of synonyms to pick up control words from the topic sentence and thereby to achieve coherence.

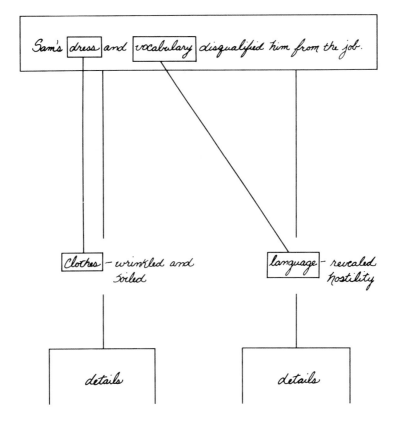

Certainly there are other transition signals that the writers might have used in these paragraphs. It is important that you use signals that indicate the beginning of a new part of the paragraph's development.

The following paragraph is a full development of the first example with details or examples at all levels of support. The transition signals are boxed. Notice how they help tie the paragraph parts together.

I can think of three things that stand out in my mind as especially noteworthy. First, the plot was awful. It was one of those trite when-will-we-ever-find-happiness-as-long-as-you-are-a-priest stories told "against a backdrop of mystery and intrigue." What mystery? What intrigue? How mysterious and intriguing can western Wisconsin be? Second, the casting showed no imagination. It was not one of the coups of the decade with Paul Newman as a bishop and Dorothy Malone as a groupie. All that was missing was Katharine Hepburn as the whorehouse madam. However, Burl Ives filled in nicely. | Third, | the violence seemed unnecessary to the plot. For a love story with a religious overtone to it, the film was far too violent. Every three or four minutes someone was being bitten by a rabid dog, socked in the eye by the mean old father-in-law, or zonked on the head with a candelabrum. An especially gruesome scene took place in the madam's garden—a garden filled with man-eating plants. That scene, of course, provided the surprise ending we all needed. This film clearly is no Academy Award contender for next year.

You can readily see that the three main divisions in the complete paragraph are tied together by transition signals that easily prepare the reader for a change. The detail sentences following each of the major divisions are minor-level supports that directly relate to the lead sentence in each category.

In using transition signals, you must be certain to select words and phrases that show the proper relationship among your paragraph parts. Some signals are almost automatic; they come naturally with certain types of paragraphs. Other signals require careful thought so that they connect the parts of your paragraph and show the proper relationship among those parts.

Here is a list of some of the most frequently used transition signals:

also	for instance	moreover	similarly
although	for one thing	nevertheless	still
but	furthermore	notwithstanding	though
especially	however	occasionally	whereas
first	in fact	on the contrary	yet
for example	in general	on the other hand	
	likewise	second	

Exercise 10

Obviously not all of the transition signals in this list have the same meaning. Some of them are used to indicate the addition of an idea, some to show the presence of an example, and some to show a contrasting idea. Use the fencepost outline on the following page to place the transition signals into their appropriate categories.

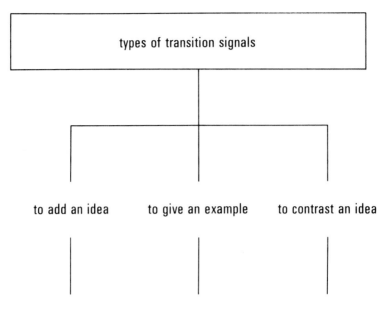

types of transition signals

to add an idea   to give an example   to contrast an idea

Exercise 11

The paragraph below offers the reader no help in seeing the relationship among ideas because the writer has used no transition signals. Rewrite the paragraph, inserting appropriate transition signals where they are needed.

Movie directors are able to make use of several techniques not available to directors of live theater. Flashbacks are very easily handled without cumbersome changes of scenes. In live theater these can sometimes be distracting. It is easy to get inside the minds of the actors, to hear their unspoken thoughts. The camera just zooms in for a closeup, and the audience hears their words but their lips don't move. In live theater the actor usually looks directly at the audience and speaks these lines. The audience may sometimes confuse these private thoughts with the other dialogue of the play. Movies can have an extravagant array of settings. It is easy to film almost any setting—mountains, beaches, or the inside of buildings—and use those sequences as backdrops for the action. Live theater requires elaborate handpainted scenes. These are often very heavy and must be moved about several times during the performance. Movie directors thus have greater flexibility than live theater can offer in the uses of flashbacks, unspoken thoughts, and setting.

Exercise 12

Select one topic sentence below. Using the model given at the top of page 83, sketch a fencepost outline for your paragraph.

1. I never get tired of being with my two best friends.
2. The salesman's intense anger was demonstrated by his words and his actions.
3. The kind of person I like to date has three basic characteristics.
4. My favorite popular music has a distinct rhythm and a happy message.
5. Our community can no longer ignore its two major social injustices and continue to prosper.

Exercise 13

Now write your completed paragraph, based on the structural scheme that you have designed.

Another way to develop coherence in your paragraph is to use ideas that constantly link back to the controlling idea in the topic sentence. Repeating the key idea in your topic sentence and throughout your paragraph will emphasize that idea and help to keep the parts of the paragraph interlocked.

The devices of structural repetition that you have just studied are generally used at the major level of support, the level at which you ordinarily indicate the important divisions of your paragraph. *Repetition of the controlling idea*, on the other hand, may be used at any level of support. The transition signals you might use for this type of repetition are very often not indicated directly by the topic sentence. In such instances, you must develop signals according to your main idea for organizing the paragraph. Here are some examples.

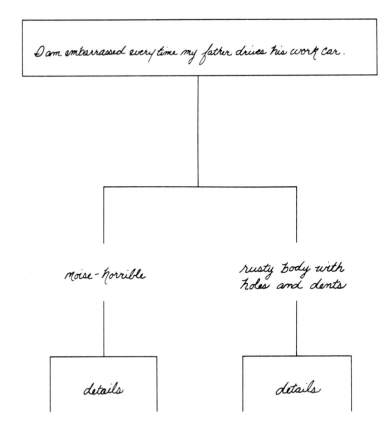

The words *noise* and *rusty body* directly relate to the writer's embarrassment concerning her father's work car by explaining exactly what embarrasses her.

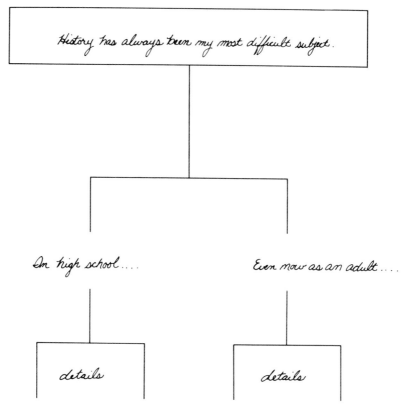

In this example, the writer plans to emphasize the word *always* in the topic sentence by writing about two distinct times in his life.

The following examples, both excerpts from *The Lincoln Nobody Knows* by Richard N. Current, illustrate effective use of repetition of the controlling idea. Notice how the details in the first paragraph give emphasis to the key idea in the topic sentence: Lincoln "seemed taller than he was."

His figure (as many an observer saw him) was so proportioned that he seemed taller than he was, especially when he wore his high silk hat. His head, atop a long, scraggy neck with a conspicuous Adam's apple, appeared to be small for the rest of him. His chest was thin and narrow in comparison with the long, bony arms that hung at his side, the giant's hands, the long, bony legs, the oversized feet.

All of the details in the following paragraph support the key idea in the topic sentence: Lincoln "walked with a firm and even tread."

He stood with a slight stoop and walked with a firm and even tread. "He steps slowly and deliberately, almost always with his head inclined forward and his hands clasped behind his back," a *Chicago Tribune* reporter wrote. Herndon, who had more opportunities to observe, put the matter more precisely as well as more picturesquely: "The inner sides of his feet were parallel, if not a little pigeontoed. He did not walk cunningly—Indian like, but cautiously and firmly. In walking, Mr. Lincoln put the whole foot flat down on the ground at once —not lifting himself from the toes, and hence had no spring or snap ...to his walk."

As a beginning writer, you should make extensive use of repetition of your controlling idea. Be certain that each of your sentences at the major support level repeats in some way the idea of the topic sentence, and be certain that sentences at the detail levels support the idea of the sentence that they modify.

Exercise 14

In a manner similar to that used in the two Lincoln paragraphs above, circle all of the words and phrases that contribute to the coherence of this paragraph:

Sports-car owners are a brand-new breed of sports bores and, in order of prevalence, I would put them in third place. I have noticed more and more of my acquaintances who nowadays will stop everything to discuss the advantages (social and stylistic) and disadvantages (economic) of wire wheels. The sound of a single word, floating out of a distant conversation in a crowded room, is sufficient to alert the wary bore watcher to the sports-car bore. The word is "downshift" or "downshifting." In another era most drivers shifted up (there *were* some down-shifters even then, but not many, and the practice was called "double clutching"). Now hardly anybody shifts at all except for the sports-car bore who never mentions how he gets *up* into high gear but will talk for hours on how he gets *down* out of it. It takes something like the old Notre Dame shift to avoid him....

—Stephen Birmingham, "A Bore Watcher's Guide"

Exercise 15

Select a paragraph that you have already written and circle the words or phrases that contribute to coherence. If the paragraph lacks appropriate coherence, rewrite it by inserting words or phrases to make it cohere; then circle those words or phrases.

Exercise 16

The sentences in the following paragraph have been scrambled. Rearrange them into a coherent order and write the paragraph. Pay attention to transition words and phrases to find your major clues. You might even wish to make a fencepost outline of the paragraph first.

_____ To be the pilot of one of those planes that zoomed quickly beyond the clouds became my dream.

_____ I still remember my thrill as that giant jet lifted off the runway.

_____ Five years later I took my first flying lesson.

_____ I spent all of my money on those lessons, sometimes flying three or four times a week until I got my own license.

_____ All of my life I have wanted to be an airline pilot.

_____ I used to go there with my older brother to watch the planes take off and land.

_____ I doubt that I have been that excited since then, not even when I later flew a plane myself.

_____ Bit by bit I am moving closer to my dream of becoming an airline pilot.

_____ When I was about eight years old, my family lived near a medium-sized airport.

_____ I don't think I took my eyes away from the window view the entire time of the three-hour flight.

_____ Once we were in the air and the instructor let me make some simple turns, I felt I could conquer almost anything.

_____ Now I am taking instruction to become a commercial pilot.

_____ It was all even more exciting than I had imagined as the craft filled with dozens of passengers and the pilot welcomed us.

_____ I was thirteen when I took my own first ride in a plane.

_____ I just know that I will make it.

_____ I don't know if I was more scared or excited as I sat for the first time behind the controls.

CHAPTER

5 Patterns for Organization

Up to this point, you have been studying material that enables you to structure a paragraph with distinct levels of support to achieve unity and with sufficient devices of repetition to achieve coherence. Now you will begin to learn some of the specific methods of giving order to the various sentences and ideas that make up your paragraph.

Not every paragraph is designed to accomplish the same purpose. One paragraph tells of an experience, another gives directions, one argues an important idea, and so on. You must select a method of paragraph organization to fit your intended purpose.

Exercise 1

You probably make frequent use of the traditional patterns for organization, sometimes without even realizing that you are making several major statements of support. Below are three different topic sentences, each followed by several major statements of support. Number the support statements in the order in which you would probably use them in the paragraph. Following each paragraph is a space in which you can indicate why you grouped ideas in the sequence that you selected.

1. After I get up in the morning, my world is filled with frantic activities as I try to get myself ready for the day.

    _____ My next action is to throw on old clothes, sometimes those I wore the day before, and take the dogs out for a morning walk.

_____ I jump out of bed when the alarm rings and head directly for my morning shower.

_____ Finally, I gather my books and class notes and leave for campus.

_____ When we return, the dogs get fed and I have a quick breakfast.

_____ Then it is time to redress, this time putting on clean, fresh clothes that are suitable for school and work.

Reason for arrangement: _____

2. One of these days I am going to have to settle down and devote a full day to cleaning my closet.

_____ Another reason is that I can no longer find things amid the terrible clutter.

_____ The most important reason is that the closet is so crowded that I cannot put another thing in there, not even one more shirt.

_____ Also, the boxes on the top shelf are so jammed together that I am afraid some of my good shoes are getting squashed.

_____ I am also a bit concerned that my mother will start to yell even more loudly if I don't get it cleaned soon.

Reason for arrangement: _____

3. As we entered the picnic area, the sight overwhelmed us with its beauty.

_____ In the distance, the towering mountains capped with peaks of snow framed the entire picture.

_____ Farther out on the lake we could see dozens of sailboats, many with multicolored sails dancing in the light wind.

_____ The beach area was filled with hundreds of people busying themselves with swimming, sunning, or just plain people-watching.

_____ The three picnic huts, each just off the road, were rustic replicas of old country estates.

Reason for arrangement: _____

ORDER OF IMPORTANCE

One of the most useful ways to organize a paragraph is by *order of importance*. This pattern is most helpful because it provides a guide to your teacher that will let him or her see the process of your thinking. You do the sorting and arranging so your reader will not have to guess what you consider to be important.

In the typical paragraph arranged according to this model, you structure your supporting sentences in such a way that they move from the *most important* to the *least important*. This is a popular method of organization because hurried readers often stop partway through a paragraph. With this pattern of organization, these readers will still see your major points. You may find it convenient to think of such a paragraph as an inverted triangle:

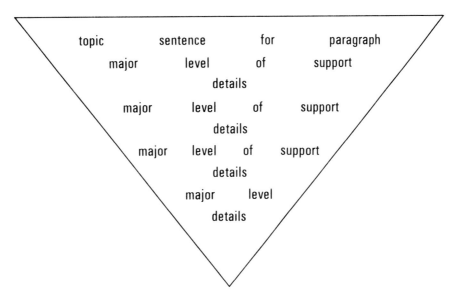

Here is a sample paragraph:

I am finally going to trade my old car this weekend. I really hate to get rid of it after all of these years, but the transmission is now completely shot. I cannot shift from second to third anymore, so I have to go chugging along the highway at 45 in second gear. The car also needs a new muffler and tailpipe. Last week the tailpipe fell off on the freeway and nearly caused an accident. Too, the convertible top is in bad condition. Two weeks ago I parked the car in the driveway overnight, and a bad hailstorm tore two large holes and several small ones in the top. Finally, I have to get rid of the car because none of my friends will go riding with me anymore. Not only do they hate to be seen in such a pitiful looking wreck, but they also never know whether they will get where they are going. All in all, I guess it's bye-bye car.

Sometimes the nature of your topic or your particular purpose for writing to a given audience will suggest that you might want to reverse the order and move from the least important to the most important. This pattern, still organization according to importance, is called *climactic organization*. It is very useful when you have a particularly clever or punchy comment to make about your most important reason. It is also often useful when you are asking your reader to take some kind of action—to agree with you, contribute money, sign a petition, and so forth—as a result of your argument. Then you certainly want to save your strongest reason so that it will come closest to your appeal for action.

A paragraph organized in this manner requires the reader to read all the way through to know the full meaning. The structural scheme for the paragraph looks much like this:

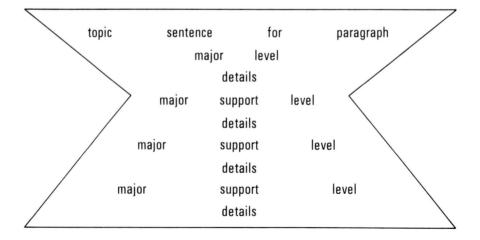

Here is a sample paragraph:

> I am going to trade in my car this weekend. My girl does not like the color. She says that an orange and blue finish just does not go with her hair. Too, the top is in bad condition. Last week I parked the car in the driveway overnight, and a bad hail storm left the convertible top in shreds. I also need a new tailpipe. Yesterday on the turnpike the old one fell off and nearly caused a ten-car pileup. But I guess the thing that finally convinced me that old Bertha was ready for the junk yard was the transmission. I can't shift from second to third anymore, so I have to go chugging along the highway at 45 in second gear.

Moving the Topic Sentence

Thus far you have begun with a topic sentence and developed your paragraph by offering supporting details. This movement from the general to the specific is perhaps the one you will want to use most often. However, there are times when you will want to reverse that sequence and move from the specific to the general.

This type of structure gives you the first opportunity in this text to write a paragraph with a topic sentence in a position other than at the beginning. Do not relax your attention to unity—every detail in the paragraph still must support the topic sentence, and the topic sentence must be stated. Only the most sophisticated writer can produce a good paragraph with an implied topic sentence.

In the example that follows, Charles Dickens describes one of his characters. Notice how he begins by listing specific details that all point toward the topic sentence: "Miss Murdstone was a metallic lady."

> It was Murdstone who was arrived, and a *gloomy-looking* lady she was; *dark*, like her brother, whom she greatly resembled in face and voice; and with very *heavy* eyebrows, nearly meeting over her large nose, as if, being disabled by the wrongs of her sex from wearing *whiskers*, she had carried them to that account. She brought with her two uncompromising *hard black boxes*, with her initials on the lids in *hard brass nails*. When she paid the coachman she took her money out

of a *hard steel purse*, and she kept the purse in a very *jail* of a bag which hung upon her arm by a *heavy chain*, and *shut up* like a *bite*. I had never, at that time, seen such a *metallic* lady altogether as Miss Murdstone was. [Emphasis added.]

—Charles Dickens, *David Copperfield*

In the following paragraph, the author begins by presenting specific pieces of evidence that all become important for an understanding of the rather dramatic final (topic) sentence.

> When Frank first slithered up beside me in the library and asked to see my sociology homework, I didn't think much about it. Later I discovered tht he submitted a copy of my book review for his own homework. Still, I wanted to trust him. I was not even suspicious when he moved to sit across the aisle from me in our data processing class. It was Mr. Rodriguez, our instructor, who detected his wandering eyes that time. Two weeks later I noticed that Frank wasn't doing any of the activities required in chemistry lab. Instead, he was wandering around the room making mental notes of the results other students were getting so he could write his report. Although I like to think positively about others, I had to face the hard fact. Frank was a cheat!

Whether you begin with the topic sentence and add supporting details or begin with the details and end with the topic sentence, you must keep in mind that you are arranging information in a distinct order of importance. Use words or phrases that help your reader see the relationship among your paragraph parts. Some useful transition markers are these:

first, second, third
one reason, another reason, a final reason
the most, the least
next
almost of equal importance
even more important
last
finally

Much of the writing that you will do in college and throughout life will be organized according to a sequence of importance. The following are but a few of the instances in which you might use such a pattern:

1. to justify an idea or opinion
2. to summarize an issue or problem
3. to argue a point
4. to present reactions to a stimulus
5. to compare two or more items

Exercise 2

Clip from your local newspaper an article about which you have very strong feelings, either positive or negative. Write a paragraph that might serve as a letter to the editor. State your general reaction to the situation described in the article (you agree, disagree, violently oppose, or support). Structure your topic sentence and your paragraph so that you clearly have three or four specific levels of support, each with detail. Use a fencepost outline similar to the following to structure your ideas. Remember that you may have more than three major levels of support.

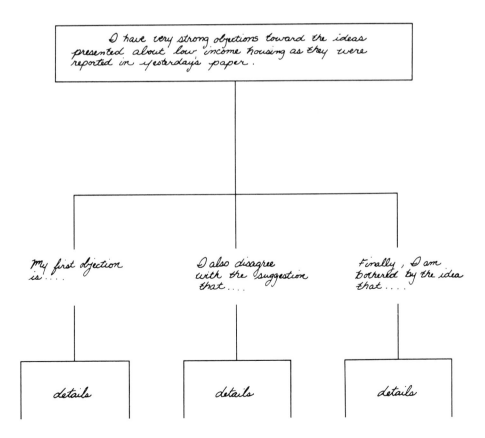

Following are some general statements that you might develop into paragraphs. Select one that interests you; then, on a separate sheet of paper, develop a working scheme similar to the one above. Write a finished paragraph based on your working plan.

1. The party last night was simply horrible.

2. I think that _____ is the most important invention of this century.

3. It is really time for me to get away for a short vacation.

4. Somehow I have got to find a way to earn more money.

5. I hope I never see my ex-friend _____ again!

Exercise 4

Rewrite the paragraph, this time using climactic order. You may wish to reword some of your sentences. You will probably want to rephrase your topic sentence so it fits better into the final position.

Exercise 5

Write a paragraph using the topic sentence given below as the concluding sentence. Structure the beginning of your paragraph so that it contains major and minor levels of support leading to the topic sentence.

Topic sentence: All of this evidence was enough for me—I put down my money and bought a (name of car, radio, clothing, or some similar item).

Exercise 6

A type of writing that very often uses climactic order is one that describes someone or something and ends with a striking comment about the person or thing that serves to pull all of the earlier details together. Charles Dickens' description of Miss Murdstone (pages 97–98) is an example of this type of writing.

Look at the following examples and think how you might complete them by filling in appropriate names of people or things in the blank spaces. Select one of the sentences and write a climactically ordered paragraph that will lead to your completed sentence as its conclusion.

1. _____ is certainly the most boring person I've ever met.

2. _____ always dresses like he (or she) is a circus clown.

3. I've never known anyone quite so in love with himself (or herself) as

_____ .

4. My _____ at home simply looks like a disaster area.

5. My cousin's _____ must definitely be the most unusually decorated one in this city.

ORDER OF TIME

Another effective method for organizing material within a paragraph is to make use of *chronological order*. Chronological order is *time* order. In a paragraph organized according to this method, you arrange details in the order in which they occurred, almost always moving from the first event to the most recent. The signal words that you use are those that signify shifts in time.

Your paragraph may focus on any type of time measurement: minutes, hours, days, weeks, years. You should attempt to use signal words that make the reader aware of the time movement but that do not call undue attention to themselves. That is, do not begin every sentence with expressions such as

"For two more hours," "During the next ten minutes," or "Five minutes later." You might wish to use transition words such as these:

first, second, third	in preparation
next	following that step
after	until
afterward	while
then	when
before	a bit later
later	as soon as
now	

Look at the following paragraph, which gives directions for getting from one place to another. Notice how each new step in the procedure is introduced by a transition marker.

> Getting from our campus to downtown requires about thirty-five minutes and some careful planning. First you have to go to the east campus exit and wait for the #82 bus. It comes by about every twenty minutes. After you have boarded the bus, you can relax for a full ten minutes. It goes beyond the apartment buildings and enters the freeway at the Wayside Entrance. As soon as it crosses Hillview Lane, you need to pull the signal for a stop. You exit at the next stop, which is Broadview Station. Then you wait about ten minutes more until the #151 bus comes along. It is an express that will go directly into the heart of downtown. When you are safely aboard #151, you can relax; your problems are over. Now all you have to do is remember which of the three downtown stops you want.

The following paragraph uses time organization to explain what has happened to the writer during the day and why she is so tired.

> When I finally get off work tonight, I will barely be able to stagger home and fall into the bed. It all began when my alarm went off at 5:30 this morning. I was fresh then, and I bounced out of bed, showered, and made a quick cup of coffee. The coffee started my problems. I accidentally spilled the entire cup on the bed while I was dressing. Without much free time at all, I then had to change all of the bed linens

and put the top sheet, which had a huge brown coffee stain on it, in to soak. As soon as I had done that, the telephone rang. Mr. Meyer, the elderly man who lives upstairs, called to say that he was sick and to ask if I would take his dog out for a walk. There went another fifteen minutes. By the time I got to work, I was already half-tired and totally frustrated. Then my supervisor asked me if I would hand-deliver a special requisition to our stationery supplier five blocks away. A bit later Jim, my friend who works in the billing department, stopped by to ask if I could help him rearrange his filing system. After this task was completed, I got a call telling me that the stationery order was ready; thus I had another five-block walk each way. And I had to carry three heavy boxes back, too. Following that trip, I settled down to my own desk and my own work. But as soon as I was settled the phone rang and Mrs. Paulley said that she had a doctor's appointment and that I would have to answer her phone as well as mine. So far I have had eighteen phone calls, all requiring me to go to the file and find the right folder with the right information for the caller. It is now 4:45, and I have only fifteen minutes to go. Then I will head home, turn off my phone, crawl between my clean sheets, and collapse.

You may use paragraphs organized by time patterns for many different purposes. Listed are some of the principal reasons for writing that make use of time-ordered sequences:

1. to tell a story or experience
2. to give directions
3. to give instructions
4. to review a book or movie
5. to summarize historical events
6. to report on the action(s) of an individual or an organization

Exercise 7

Think about what happens to you on a typical morning from the time you wake up until you get to school or to work. Use a structural plan similar to the one on the following page to organize your thoughts, but remember that you may have more than three time blocks. After you have structured your thoughts in a time sequence, write your finished paragraph. Be certain to offer specific details to explain what happens to you at each different time block.

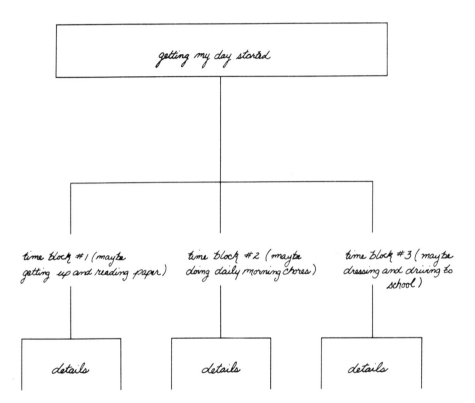

getting my day started

time block #1 (maybe getting up and reading paper)

time block #2 (maybe doing daily morning chores)

time block #3 (maybe dressing and driving to school)

details

details

details

Exercise 8

Using a fencepost outline similar to the one above, structure and write a paragraph telling about the most memorable day of your life. How did it begin? What series of events occurred? Don't tell everything; rather, select highlights of the day that will show your reader why it was so memorable. Use transition words to move the reader along from one time sequence to another.

Exercise 9

Structure and write a paragraph that briefly summarizes the action in a movie you have recently seen or a book you have recently read. Begin with a topic sentence indicating the general mood of the movie or book. Was it humorous, frightening, boring, exciting, depressing? Block the action into large time chunks for the major levels of support. Describe one or two specific incidents that occurred at each time block.

ORDER OF SPACE

If the purpose of your writing is to describe how something looks, your most effective organization pattern is usually that of *space*. Try to see yourself, the writer, as a camera. From what vantage point can you best see the item? What details do you wish to emphasize? How will you arrange those details?

Rather than jumping from one place to another, the writing should follow the movement that you might imagine a movie camera would make, carefully and systematically describing objects according to a predetermined order. There are several general methods of movement, each effective in particular situations.

from the near to the faraway
from the faraway to the near

from the left to the right
from the right to the left

from the top to the bottom
from the bottom to the top

from the inside to the outside
from the outside to the inside

from the obvious to the unobvious
from the unobvious to the obvious

The plan that you use will depend in part upon the object that you are describing and in part upon the emphasis that you wish to make. For example, if you are describing an unusually tall building—the Empire State Building in New York or the Sears Tower in Chicago—you will probably use a top-to-bottom sequence. If you are describing your car, you might want to use a left-to-right movement. If you want to capture your initial response as you walk into a large church or synagogue, you will probably use near to far as your ordering system.

The most important thing to remember when writing a paragraph involving spatial development is that your movement from scene to scene must be systematic and orderly. In describing a room, for example, you do not jump from details about the walls to the furniture to the curtains to the lighting fixtures to the floor. You move systematically from item to item in a prearranged plan.

When you are writing according to spatial order, you focus your attention on the *location* of objects and their physical relationship with other objects. In chronological order, you use signal words and major-level support to indicate shifts in time. In spatial order, you use signal words and major-level support to indicate location. You focus upon where an object is located in relation to other objects.

Remember that the purpose of spatial writing is to describe something physically. Make certain that your control word is a "picture word," that is, something that you can take a picture of. You cannot take a picture of attitudes: George has a *nice* personality, or Mary was the *kindest* person I have ever known.

Your major support sentences are usually those that move from one point of attention to another—from one camera shot to another. For these sentences, it is extremely important for you to provide transitions to show your reader exactly where you are moving. Some typical transition signals are:

up, down	just above, behind
beside	closer, farther
to the left, to the right	in the distance
next to	higher, lower

When you are thinking about the structure of your paragraph, each major support sentence on your fencepost outline as being a picture of the whole setting that you are describing. You can then re___ the transition signals you need to use to move your reader along from one scene (picture) to another.

After reading the paragraph describing Professor Wilbert's office (page 108), one student developed the following fencepost outline to describe her sister's bedroom.

fr. p. 78

My sister keeps her room so clean and orderly that I get nervous everytime I go in there.

next to the bed — to the left of the desk

her bed and nightstand | her desk and study area | her closet

bed always made | only one book and lamp on stand | dusted and fluffed daily | books in neat stacks on corner | pencils sharp and ready | "to do" list by lamp | polished daily | shoes in their boxes | clothes hung in color-coordinated groups

Look carefully at the following example of spatial development. Notice how the details all support the control word and how, too, transition signals help move the reader along from one point of focus to another.

Professor Wilbert's office is easily the junkiest room that I have ever seen. To the left of the door, she has a standing coatrack. The last time I looked at it I counted two sweaters, a light summer coat, three winter scarves, her heavy winter coat, and six umbrellas. Every item was hanging carelessly on the rack as though it had been thrown there from five feet away. Beside the rack is a chair that is supposed to be used by students who come for conferences. But it is always filled with books, files, or papers waiting to be graded. Her desk sits next to this chair and is another mass of objects. There are more books, files, and papers, but there are also pictures of six members of her family, two very dirty coffee mugs, a bowl of very stale candy, her sandwich for the day, and a collection of newspapers from the last month or so. One pile of reports on the corner of her desk is easily twenty inches high. Just behind her desk is a huge bulletin board. She puts everything there and removes nothing. There are announcements, news clippings, two letters from the dean, a note to write to her brother in Akron, and a letter notifying her that she has been given an award for excellent teaching. That notice, yellowed now, is six years old. The window just to the right of her bulletin board is cluttered with plants, about half of them dead in their pots. The live ones reach awkwardly toward the sun, tangling themselves through the broken slats of the venetian blinds. She is an excellent teacher, but I do not see how Professor Wilbert can work in so junky an office.

Exercise 10

Underline the major support sentences in the paragraph above and circle the transition words that move the reader from one scene to another.

The details that you elect to use in your spatial writing will be those that directly support the control word in your topic sentence. If your topic sentence promises to talk about the majestic height of a structure, you need not pause to write about the color of the brick. If your topic sentence suggests emphasis upon the disorganization of a room, you will not necessarily write about the room's size. You select only those details that develop the emphasis suggested by your topic sentence. Then you arrange them into a formal spatial order.

Paragraphs developed according to spatial organization r
when you wish to describe any of the following:

1. a person
2. a scene
3. an object
4. the relationship in space of one object to another

Exercise 11

Just for review, underline the control word(s) in each of the following topic sentences (review pages 74–75 if you need to refresh your memory).

1. Everything about the living room reflected elegance.
2. Somehow Mary's face always suggested her comic personality.
3. The exterior of the house clearly indicated its melancholy role in the neighborhood.
4. No matter what you say, Sir Joshua is the ugliest dog that I have ever seen.
5. He looked absolutely splendid in his tuxedo.
6. The inside of the antique shop was crowded with clutter.
7. She always wears the wildest clothes to parties.
8. I will never forget the beautiful colors of the sunrise over the lake.
9. Everything in his small room was faded and old.
10. The fall colors along the trail through the woods were varied and gorgeous.

Exercise 12

You have been asked to help a college committee prepare a booklet that will be used to promote the college; your task is to write a positive description of some of the most important buildings or settings on campus. Think about your task. What campus scenes would you most likely emphasize in such a booklet? What details would you use for each scene? What kind of "camera movement" would you use to move from one scene to the next?

You might wish to use a fencepost outline somewhat like the following one to organize your ideas. Don't forget to include specific details for each scene that you list, and remember that your own description may include more than the three major support sentences (separate scenes) indicated in the example. Write your own finished paragraph based on the organizational plan that you have developed.

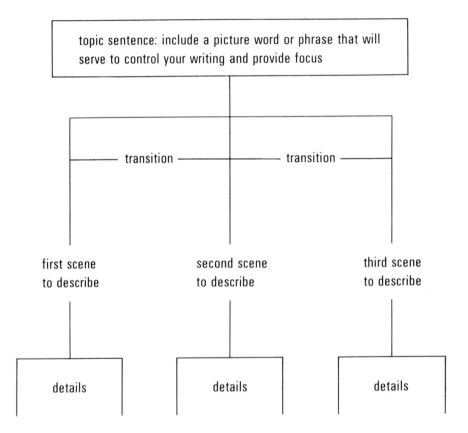

Exercise 13

You are aware that there are often several ways of looking at the same object. This time, assume that you are a member of a student committee that is writing a letter to the college administration pointing out some of the ugliest sights on your campus. If you were writing such a letter, what three or four specific sights on your campus would you mention to your college administration? What details would you include for each sight?

Prepare yourself a working scheme somewhat like the one on page 110. Include a very negative word such as *ugly* in your topic sentence. Write your finished paragraph based on the working model that you develop.

Exercise 14

Select one of the broad topics listed below and develop it into a paragraph that is spatially organized. Remember that your purpose is to describe. Use a picture word in your topic sentence and include specific details at each level of your paragraph that will reinforce that picture word.

broad topics

1. your favorite hideaway
2. the inside of your favorite restaurant
3. the inside of a church or synagogue
4. the favorite room in your home
5. your mother or father on Sunday morning

C H A P T E R

6 Types of Development

Now that you are familiar with the different ways that ideas within a paragraph may be organized (by importance, time, and space) to support the topic sentence, you should begin to practice some of the different strategies for developing your paragraphs toward a specific purpose.

You write to accomplish a purpose: to illustrate by giving an example, to classify ideas, to give directions or instructions, to compare and/or contrast, to explain how something works or why some situation exists, and so on. For each of these different purposes you need different strategies for development.

As you work through the sections in this unit, remember that the types of development studied here are independent from the three methods of organization studied in the previous unit. That is, you have to make a choice about each one—organization and development—when you write. You might, for instance, write a paragraph that is developed by illustration, but that paragraph might be organized by importance, time, or space. You would select the organizational method that best fits your topic, but that method may obviously change from paragraph to paragraph or topic to topic.

ILLUSTRATION

One of the most frequently used strategies for developing ideas is *illustration*. Often you find yourself supporting a point that you are attempting to make by giving an example to illustrate that point. You even lead in to your example by using a phrase such as "Let me give you an example" or "Let me show you." Developing an idea by illustration is a very natural process and a relatively easy one.

When you develop by illustration, your task is to give specific support to the idea suggested in the topic sentence. The key word is *specific*. You must give your reader an example that will be definite. An important idea to remember is "show, don't tell." Your topic sentence tells your reader a fact— for instance, that the local baseball team is not doing well because of incompetent management. After writing that topic sentence, your next task is to show by specific example how incompetent management has caused the team to perform inadequately.

Many paragraphs developed by illustration make use of a narrative process. You will usually find yourself recounting an experience, or perhaps a series of experiences, that supports your main (topic) idea. Once you have a main idea, your next task is to find an incident or a series of related incidents that you might be able to use to support that idea.

You may develop your topic by using one extended illustration or several shorter ones. Here are two paragraphs about the local baseball team. Paragraph A uses one illustration, and paragraph B uses three short ones.

Paragraph A

If the manager of our team does not learn how to get along with people, the team may never win another game. Last night, again, he arrived at the park with a chip on his shoulder. This time Chuck Schaum, the catcher, was his target. He chewed Chuck out for missing a throw to second the night before; then he jumped on him for not doing well in batting practice. When Chuck tried to say something, he was told, "Shut up, and just stay out of my way tonight!" By that time the other players, who had overheard all of the squabbling, were so tense that no one felt like playing ball.	**topic sentence** **one specific incident retold** **concluding statement**

Paragraph B

If the manager of our team does not learn how to get along with people, the team may never win another game. Last night Chuck Schaum, the	**topic sentence**

ILLUSTRATION   113

catcher, was his target. He bawled Chuck out for **first illustration** missing a throw to second the night before, and then for not doing well in batting practice. Earlier in the afternoon he had had a rift with one of the **second illustration** sports reporters. Calling the reporter from the team's dressing room, he claimed the story in the morning paper was a lie and that the reporter was ignorant and prejudiced. He then challenged him to a fight on the parking lot after the game that night. Two days ago his target was not one of his players **third illustration** or the reporters but the fans. He angrily ran from the dugout to the seats behind first base and began exchanging profanities with some fans there. Only the restraining efforts of two players and an umpire kept him from climbing into the stands and exchanging fisticuffs. Obviously not many people are **concluding statement** in the mood to play effective baseball in such a potentially explosive atmosphere.

Think about Paragraph B in terms of a fencepost outline. You can quite easily see that it contains three major support sentences (the three illustrations), each followed by several sentences of detail. If you look at the sequence of the three illustrations, you can also easily see that this writer has organized his material by time and has used reverse chronological order.

Whether you use one extended illustration or a series of shorter illustrations to prove your topic sentence depends upon the specific situation and just how much information you have. Sometimes you can make a better case for your position if you have several separate but related pieces of information. For example, no one would lose patience with the ball club manager because of one incident, but he might be fired because of repeated incidents such as those detailed in paragraph B. At other times you might better support your idea if you can give extensive detail about just one incident.

Remember the advice "Show, don't tell." Include sufficient specific facts in your paragraph to make it interesting. Your goal is to involve the reader in the illustration you are presenting so that he or she will agree with the idea in your topic sentence.

If you do elect to develop an idea by using several separate but related incidents, you must make a decision regarding the organization of the incidents. Chronological organization is one possible scheme (paragraph B makes use of reverse chronological order), but moving from the most important fact to the least important is also an effective method. Be certain to use appropriate transition signals that will help your reader see the relationship among the incidents that you illustrate.

E.B. White was for years one of America's most popular essay writers. In the following paragraph, he offers two support ideas for what he describes as the "violence around here." What are those two support ideas? What about this paragraph makes you feel that White is having fun with his topic and is not terribly concerned about the *violence* he suggests as his topic?

> There has been a certain amount of violence around here this spring, not counting Nancy's children. Our chimney got hit by lightning in April, and I blew the furnace up in May. It was time for it to blow up, I guess. Anyway, it proved easy work. All I had to do was chuck in a piece of an old plank, on top of a wood fire, and away she went. Made a dandy noise. I guess there was a little dynamite or something buried in the plank. I still have some of the same plank left, and the next time I use it on the fire I am going to stand further away. The insurance adjuster was down from Bangor to case the joint, and he seemed impressed by the infinite variety of my disasters. The chimney looked like an act of God, but the furnace looked exactly like an act that I would be likely to put on, judging from my appearance. After a little talk, he had me pretty well convinced that I had no business chucking stuff into my own furnace, and I got the impression that he felt God was rather cheeky, too, fooling around with a brick chimney that was out of his territory....

Sometimes you may be so certain of the importance of a particular incident to your main idea (topic sentence) that you do not explain it carefully enough to your reader. Remember that the incidents used to illustrate your topic sentence must be related and that it is your responsibility as the writer to show that relationship to your reader.

Below is a topic sentence with the control word boxed. Following the topic sentence is a list of ideas that a student proposed to include for illustration.

ILLUSTRATION   115

Mr. Hull's accounting class was easily the most ⌐difficult⌐ course I
have ever taken.
> lengthy homework assignments
> rigid two-hour exams
> eight o'clock in the morning
> highly detailed

When the student wrote the rough draft of his paragraph, his third incident
read like this:

> The class met at eight o'clock in the morning. It seems to me that I have
> always disliked early-morning classes.

Although the idea may have been clear in the student's mind, he did nothing
to help the reader see the relationship between the class's difficulty and its
eight o'clock time. After some discussion with the instructor, the student
rewrote that part of the paragraph as follows.

> The class met at eight o'clock in the morning. I work until midnight every
> night and have to get up by 6 A.M. to make an 8 A.M. class. I was always
> sleepy in Mr. Hull's class, and my mind simply refused to tune in to the
> highly detailed thinking that the course required.

Illustration as a method of development is used by writers in a wide
variety of fields. Historians use it to document a fact about a particular battle,
ministers use it to make a theological concept clearer and more realistic, and
business executives use it to justify a specific action within their realm of
supervision. But in every instance, the reader must be able to see the
relationship between the illustration and the topic sentence; otherwise the
effort is lost.

Exercise 1

Below are three topic sentences for illustration paragraphs, followed by
a list of possible illustrations. Circle the control word in each topic sentence
and mark an X beside the example that will need the most careful work to
have a clear relationship to the topic sentence. Write that part of the
paragraph (two to four sentences) in the space provided.

A. After six months, I am finally beginning to enjoy my job.
　　　more relaxed with my boss
　　　greater feeling of confidence
　　　fifteen percent raise

B. Television has had a bad effect on my family's home life.
　　　no conversation
　　　meals eaten in front of set
　　　arguments over what to watch

C. Although Susan liked it very much, I was not interested in the novel at all.
　　　over 500 pages long
　　　dislike Civil War stories
　　　too much introduction before real story began

ILLUSTRATION　117

Exercise 2

Below are listed several topic sentences. Focus your attention on one of these and develop it into a paragraph by discussing *one incident* that will serve as an illustration.

1. The types of television shows that I watch indicate some of my special interests.
2. For once in my life, I was totally speechless.
3. I have seen so much hypocrisy that I have trouble believing that anyone is sincere anymore.
4. I have never been able to keep a secret for very long.

5. _____ is the best friend I have.

Exercise 3

Use the same topic from the exercise above, but this time develop a paragraph in which you use at least *three separate incidents* to illustrate the main idea.

Using illustrations (examples) is one way to make a general idea specific. Think for a moment about some of the famous quotations that you have probably heard such as "A stitch in time saves nine," "Birds of a feather flock together," or "The early bird gets the worm." One reason that these quotations linger in our society is that each of us can think of personal examples that prove them to be true. We keep them alive by illustrating them with our own experience.

Here is a paragraph that one student wrote to illustrate a well-known quotation from Michel Montaigne.

The older I become, the more truth I find in Michel Montaigne's quotation "Saying is one thing, and doing is another." When I was a very young child, Mother would often say that someday my father would get a better job and we would move to	**topic sentence states writer's position and includes the quotation and the author's name.**

a nicer house. But my father never got a better job and we never moved. In fact, my parents still live in that same house thirty-two years later, and my father still has the same job. Mother, though, is still saying that one day all of that will change. And even as a child I was as guilty as Mother of saying and not doing. I used to always say that I would clean my room tomorrow morning, but I seldom did. I used to promise Mother that I would stop eating sweets between meals, but I always managed to stop on my way home from school for a double scoop of chocolate ice cream. And I always said I was going to study more and raise my grades, especially in algebra. But somehow talking to my friends on the phone was more fun, and I never got around to doing anything about that C— in algebra. Now that I am an adult, I still do not see much change in the old controversy between saying and doing. For over a year now, I have been saying at least once a week that I wanted to stop smoking, but I keep putting off doing it. Last summer I must have told my nine year old son a dozen times that I would take him and his friends to Six Flags one Saturday. The thought of keeping track of half a dozen kids all day at an amusement park was more than I could deal with, and I never did take them. Just yesterday my husband asked me if I would help him paint the den this weekend. I said I would, but already I am beginning to think of excuses. It is just so easy to say and so difficult to do.

First example is the writer's mother many years ago.

The second example is about the writer herself when she was a child.

The third example is about the writer herself, now an adult.

Final sentence serves as a conclusion; it summarizes the quotation and restates the author's thesis.

Exercise 4

You have probably heard some of the quotations listed below used in conversation. Select one that seems best to fit your experience and write a paragraph in which you illustrate how the quotation has been true for you.

ILLUSTRATION   119

You might want to begin with a topic sentence similar to the following: The quotation (fill in quotation here) has certainly been true in my life.

As you begin thinking about your paragraph, you must decide if you are going to use only one rather long example or include several examples to make your point. You will also need to determine how you can best organize your ideas (by importance, time, or space).

1. "One good turn deserves another." Gaius Petronius
2. "To promise not to do a thing is the surest way in the world to make a body want to do that very thing." Mark Twain
3. "Men of few words are the best men." Shakespeare
4. "Nothing can bring you peace but yourself." Ralph Waldo Emerson
5. "The friendship that can cease has never been real." St. Jerome

CLASSIFICATION

One of the most frequently used forms of development is *classification*. More and more, people like to put things into tidy groups, to think of everything as belonging to some organized system. For instance, the items in a kitchen cabinet are frequently grouped according to classifications such as vegetables, fruits, spices, and baking ingredients. Items stored in a garage may be arranged into groups such as lawn or garden tools, carpentry tools, and automotive tools.

Thus, one system for giving structure in your mind to a seeming confusion is to try to arrange the component parts into a system of classes. Think, for example, about the things you may now have in your purse or wallet. Although you may have a large number of items, you can conveniently classify them into a scheme somewhat like this:

    money-related items
      currency
      coins
      credit cards
      blank checks
    grooming items
      comb

```
    brush
    mirror
identification items
    driver's license
    college ID
    Social Security card
miscellaneous items
    address book
    letter from friend
    ticket stub
    grocery list
```

Once you have sorted the disarray of items into categories, you are better prepared to write (or think) about them because you have established a pattern of organization.

The best method for seeing the organizational pattern used in classification is to make use of an outline scheme. You should list *all* members of a particular class, and each level of your scheme should become more specialized. Here is a brief classification scheme as it might be developed:

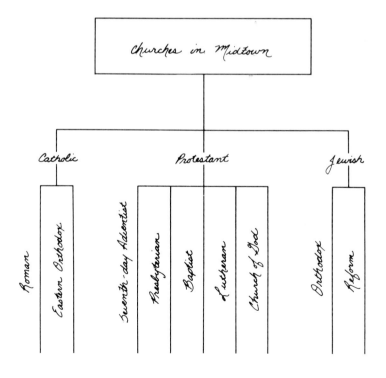

If a writer developed a paragraph from this scheme, he or she would begin with a topic sentence stating that there were three basic religious groups in Midtown. The writer would then explain or describe each group with its appropriate subdivisions.

The paragraph would need a *controlling purpose*. The purpose might be to talk about the size of the churches, their location in the city, or their attitude toward interfaith marriages. The point is that once the controlling purpose has been established, the sentences in the paragraph must develop that purpose.

The paragraph is only as valid as the scheme. If the scheme is incomplete in any part, then the writer has not properly classified the subject. A valid system of classification includes *all* members of each group. The scheme reproduced here would be invalid at the first level if an eastern religion were represented in Midtown. It would be invalid at the second level if there were also an Episcopal church in the city. Every level presented must be complete.

The following scheme is obviously incomplete.

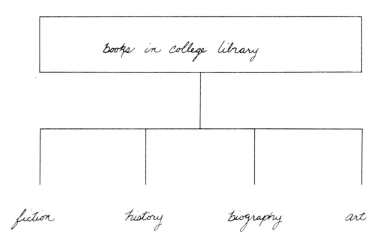

It is incomplete because it omits several obvious categories: science, reference, and geography, for example. The scheme might have been complete if it had been headed *books in my library* and if it had included a reference to all the books in the writer's personal library.

Remember two basic points about classification: (1) All levels of the scheme must be complete, and (2) your finished product should generally be proportioned in a manner similar to your scheme. For example, in the paragraph on churches in Midtown the writer would use a large amount of space discussing Protestant groups and less space discussing Catholic groups.

Here is one student's classification scheme and finished paragraph.

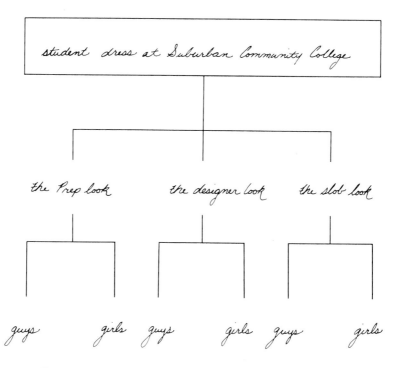

There are three types of student dress at Suburban Community College. First of all, there is the Prep look. The guys who dress in this fashion wear Lacoste shirts, khaki twill slacks, and penny loafers. When they dress up, they usually wear a navy blazer, grey slacks, a button-down shirt, and a striped silk tie. The girls who dress in this style wear Lacoste shirts, khaki skirts, and espadrilles. For a dressy look they will sport a turtleneck dress and classic pumps. Both guys and girls avoid any kind of jewelry, unless they wear a tank watch. Next is the designer look. The guys wear Ralph Lauren shirts, jeans with a variety of designer names stitched you-know-where, and strands and strands of gold peeking through the shirt that is buttoned at the waist only. Their choice of shoes leans toward the high-heeled boot. They will occasionally wear one of those chenille-looking Italian sport coats. The girls will wear silk blouses, Calvin Klein jeans, and spiked, high-heeled shoes. They often carry one of those "plastic" Louis Vuitton or Gucci bags. They wear layers of makeup, and their hair is literally plastered into place. Finally, there is the slob look. Unfortunately, most of the students dress this way. The guys will wear t-shirts with all sorts of things written on the front and back, from radio station call-letters to beer logos to suggestive sayings that would make Lenny Bruce blush. Their Levi jeans must have at least four holes in strategic places and must not be washed until worn for at least six months. A pair of dirty sneakers—Adidas, of course—is the footgear, preferably with a hole or two. The girls who dress like this are few. They tend to wear the same types of clothes, but washed; and they will often carry some sort of blue denim or canvas tote.

This paragraph is unified; the writer keeps to the framework imposed by his scheme. At each of the three major levels of his scheme, the writer provides substantial specific detail so the reader will understand just what is meant by each of the three different looks.

Exercise 5

The paragraph above was written by a student about six years ago, but types of dress on college campuses change constantly. Use the paragraph above as a rough model for your own writing, but develop your own paragraph in which you classify types of student dress currently popular on your own campus.

The following paragraph is the first paragraph in an essay by Paul Gallico entitled "A Large Number of Persons." In this first paragraph, Gallico presents almost a catalog listing of the various types of people at different athletic events. Notice that in this paragraph the classification occurs first and leads naturally to the topic sentence, which is the second to last sentence in the paragraph.

The fight crowd is a beast that lurks in the darkness behind the fringe of white light shed over the first six rows by the incandescents atop the ring, and is not to be trusted with pop bottles or other hardware. The tennis crowd is the pansy of all the great sports mobs and is always preening and shushing itself. The golf crowd is the most unwieldy and most sympathetic, and is the only horde given to mass production of that absurd noise written generally as "tsk tsk tsk tsk," and made between the tongue and teeth with head-waggings to denote extreme commiseration. The baseball crowd is the most hysterical, the football crowd the best-natured and the polo crowd the most aristocratic. Racing crowds are the most restless, wrestling crowds the most tolerant, and soccer crowds the most easily incitable to riot and disorder. Every sports crowd takes on the characteristics of the individuals who compose it. Each has its particular note of hysteria, its own little cruelties, mannerisms, and bad mannerisms, its own code of sportsman-ship and its own method of expressing its emotions.

Exercise 6

Using Gallico's paragraph as a kind of model, write your own paragraph classifying people in any of several settings that you might select. For example, you might classify people who shop at various stores, drivers along a freeway, people who have different types of pets, or any similar topic. You can observe that Gallico is having fun with his topic; try to have fun with yours, too. You might wish to follow his model and present all of your classifications and end with your topic sentence.

When you develop your classification scheme, it is important that you keep your audience and your purpose in mind. Most sets of things can be classified in a variety of ways; the one you select should be directly related to your audience and purpose. For example, if you were classifying the different grocery stores in your neighborhood and your audience was the grocery shopper on a limited budget, your purpose would be to examine the prices of the various stores. You might use major classifications such as expensive, moderate, and budget to set up your scheme. On the other hand, if you were classifying grocery stores for a gourmet cook who liked to prepare ethnic dishes, your classification scheme would focus on different ethnic foods at the various stores and might contain headings such as Indian foods, Oriental foods, Mexican foods, and so on.

Below are listed several sets of things that you could classify. Beneath each broad category, list at least two different systems for classification and indicate an audience and purpose that might be served by each system.

1. cars

system of classification   audience/purpose

system of classification   audience/purpose

2. foods

system of classification   audience/purpose

system of classification   audience/purpose

3. teachers

system of classification   audience/purpose

system of classification   audience/purpose

4. cities

system of classification   audience/purpose

system of classification   audience/purpose

5. music

system of classification   audience/purpose

system of classification   audience/purpose

You can often help your reader to understand your writing if you prepare him or her for its internal design. One way to provide this assistance is to indicate in your topic sentence the type of development that you are going to use. Paragraphs developed by classification often include words such as these in the topic sentence:

kinds   groups
types   classes
categories

Exercise 8

Write two topic sentences for each of the five items in the previous exercise. Make your sentences fit the system of classification you used and the audience or purpose you emphasized. Include in each topic sentence a word that will indicate the nature of your intended development.

Again, one of the most effective ways to organize your thoughts into a classification pattern is to group them into a fencepost outline. The paragraph about types of movies the writer disliked (page 79) came from a working outline that looked like this:

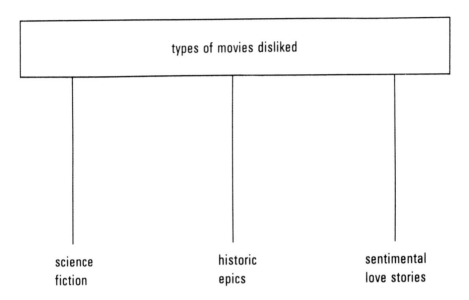

This pattern includes only major support data in the scheme. If the author had expanded the paragraph to include references to specific movie titles, the fencepost outline would have had further subdivisions similar to those in the scheme for churches in Midtown (page 121). The subdivisions would have included reference to the minor support levels necessary to develop the topic.

Exercise 9

Below are five broad subjects. For each, identify an audience and a purpose. Then prepare a classification scheme that will indicate only major support levels.

1. hobbies to enjoy at home
   audience:
   purpose:
   scheme:

2. pets that are inexpensive to own
   audience:
   purpose:
   scheme:

3. clothes that should finally be given away
   audience:
   purpose:
   scheme:

4. social gestures of charity
   audience:
   purpose:
   scheme:

5. expenses for attending college
   audience:
   purpose:
   scheme:

Exercise 10

   Select the item from the previous lists that most interests you and
develop a fencepost outline that will also include minor levels of support.
Write a finished paragraph based on the scheme that you develop.

Exercise 11

You and your family are going to move to another home and are beginning to look at various neighborhoods. What are the three or four things (schools, churches, stores, etc.) that you are most interested in having in your new locations? Write a paragraph to the Realtor who is helping you find a new home explaining these items; include details beneath each category to indicate specifically what you hope your new neighborhood will offer.

DEFINITION

Development by *definition* is a very important technique for you to master. You can readily recall arguments that started because, as you later discovered, you and another person were not defining a word or phrase in the same way. If you are debating a controversial issue, sometimes you can protect your argument by the manner in which you define key words. Throughout your life you will need to define what you mean by a specific word or phrase.

In certain types of writing, you can define simply by giving a synonym for the word in question or by briefly referring to its use.

Pulchritudinous means having physical beauty.
Someone who is *pulchritudinous* is beautiful.
To *vituperate* someone is to criticize severely or blame that individual.
A *vitriolic* comment is one that is unusually bitter or severe.
A *sphygmomanometer* is used to measure an individual's blood pressure.
A *thermostat* measures and controls temperature.

When you are using such short definitions in your writing, you must remember to define the word by using language that your audience will understand more readily than the term itself and also to avoid defining the term by using another variation of the same term. For instance, you would not say that the cylindrical object looks like a cylinder. This is an example of circular definition. If the reader knows what *cylinder* means, he or she can probably determine the meaning of *cylindrical* too.

Exercise 12

Write one-sentence definitions for each of the following words. Some lend themselves to definition by synonym and some by purpose.

1. halcyon: _____

_____

2. overt: _____

_____

3. pipette: _____

_____

4. obviate: _____

_____

5. alleviate: _____

_____

6. microfiche: _____

_____

7. kinescope: _____

_____

8. flan: _____

_____

9. chalice: _____

_____

10. canteen: _____

_____

These one-sentence definitions are often useful to give focus to a word that you use in your writing. However, more often than not you will discover that you need to do more than write one sentence to clarify a word for your reader. It will often become necessary to write one or more paragraphs in order to provide enough information for your reader to know exactly what your intended definition of a word is.

Fortunately, clear-cut patterns for writing paragraphs, or even essays, of definition exist. Although there are several possible procedures, the one most commonly used is a specialized form that first puts the word into a general class (or family) and then shows how the word is different from all other members of that class. With this form, the definition has three parts:

term—the exact word or phrase being described
class—the larger group or family to which the word is related
differences—the specific things that separate this word from all other members of its class.

Again, you will find that a variation of the fencepost outline will help you organize your thoughts before you begin to write. The simple structure looks like this:

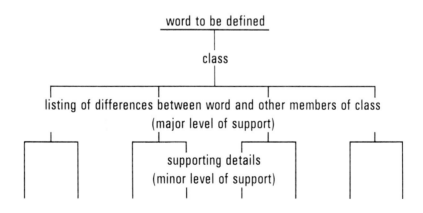

Suppose you have been asked to define a rock ballad. Your fencepost outline through the major level of support would look something like this:

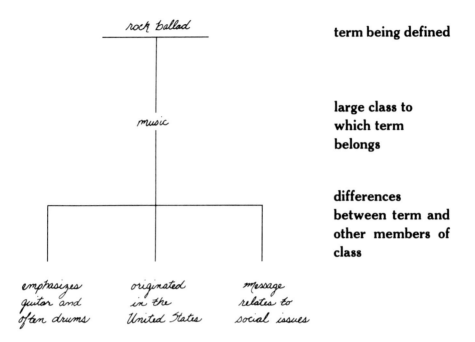

term being defined

large class to which term belongs

differences between term and other members of class

When you write your paragraph, your topic sentence would place the word in its class and suggest the differences between it and other members of that class. The major support sentences should explain the differences or indicate their importance.

Here is one student's paragraph written at the major support level only:

The rock ballad is a unique form of music that emphasizes guitars and often drums, originated in the United States, and usually relates to social themes. Unlike much other popular music, which uses the piano or horns, the rock ballad depends upon the guitar and piano for background and accompaniment. While many other types of popular music had their origins in the nightclubs of Europe, the rock ballad originated in the United

topic sentence names term, places it in class, and briefly lists differences

first major support sentence separates term from most concert-type music

second support sentence separates term from other members of class by showing place of origin

States. The words of a rock ballad song almost always relate to some broad social theme rather than to the themes of love or happiness that are often a part of much other popular music.

third support sentence shows how term differs from other members of class by its subject matter

Exercise 13

As it now stands, this paragraph validly defines a rock ballad through the major level of support. But the writer could make the paragraph more interesting and informative by including minor support sentences. Below are some minor support sentences in scrambled order. Rewrite the entire paragraph by inserting these minor support statements into appropriate positions.

The music actually developed during the 1950s.
The instruments used are almost always electronically amplified.
The lead singer most often also plays the lead guitar.
The popularity of this music has now spread throughout the world.
The message of the song is usually universal rather than personal.
A typical theme of the music is the brotherhood of all of us.
There is a distinct rhythm to the rather loud music.
Although the message is important, it is usually presented in simple
language.

The details that you include at the minor level of support are often specific. Depending upon your audience, you might want to quote some lines from a typical rock ballad, or you might want to mention some popular performers or titles.

For some paragraphs of definition, you might wish to trace the origin of the word, how it came into the language, and how it has changed meaning. Other types of details sometimes explain the specific uses of the word in various contexts and sometimes even achieve definition by explaining what the word is not.

To summarize, then, you may extend your definition by any of the following methods:

offering specific evidence
tracing history or meaning
describing physically
describing use
presenting contrasting examples.

The type of evidence that you use will depend upon the word you are defining, your audience, and your purpose.

Exercise 14

Below are three different terms for you to define. Complete each fencepost outline by placing the word in a class and by listing as many differences as you think are important.

1. a screwdriver

word

class

differences

2. a spreadsheet

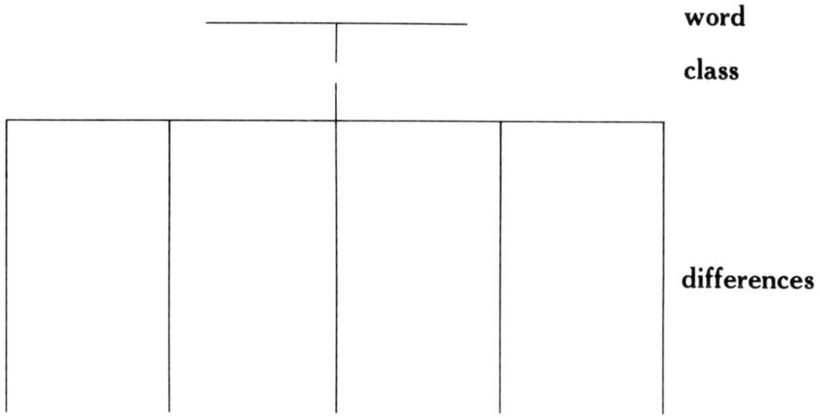

word

class

differences

3. love

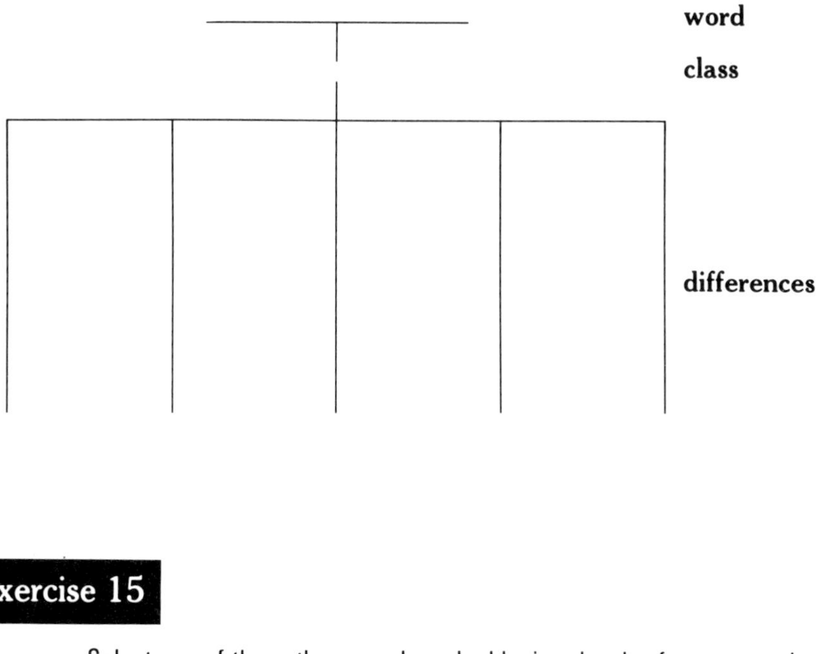

word

class

differences

Exercise 15

Select one of these three words and add minor levels of support at the appropriate places on your fencepost outline. Write the finished paragraph.

Select one of the following words or phrases for a paragraph of definition. Prepare a fencepost outline that will give structure to your writing, and consciously think about which type of evidence you will use for your minor level of support. Write your finished paragraph.

patriotism
brick
religion
country music
hockey
lonely
radical
tranquil
a word that means something special or private to you and your immediate friends

COMPARISON AND CONTRAST

Often you will find yourself faced with the task of commenting upon two or more subjects that have come to your attention. You may be deciding which of two items to buy, which of two persons to date, which of two records to play. When you arrange your ideas in such a way as to notice similarities between the objects, you are *comparing* them. When you structure your ideas so that you are aware of their differences, you are *contrasting* them. Usually the two go hand in hand. More often than not, a writer employs both comparison and contrast analysis when viewing two subjects.

It is important that objects which you compare and contrast have a natural basis for comparison. You might compare apples and oranges to explain which fruit you like better, or you might write about two different poems to evaluate which you feel most effectively treats its subject. Generally speaking, the objects that you compare or contrast should be members of the same class or family. You would not write about paper clips and playing tennis, nor would you write about goldfish and automobiles. You write about objects that have a natural relationship or that are related by the purpose of your evaluation.

When you write your comparison and contrast paragraph, organization becomes extremely important. First, to be perfectly fair, you must decide upon an absolute list of items to observe. These items must be identical for both (or all) objects you are studying. For example, if you are looking at two cars, you may decide to observe items such as size, horsepower, initial cost, cost of maintenance, and resale value. The important thing is that you look at all of these items for both cars you are considering and that you objectively gather facts for every one of these items.

After you have gathered your information according to a carefully conceived plan, you must decide how to arrange that material in your paragraph. You have two choices. Naturally you begin with a topic sentence stating your central point. Then you may present all of the material about the first car followed by all of the material about the second car. Or you may present material about the first and second cars at each level of your investigation. The following outlines indicate how you might organize your paragraph:

plan A	plan B
Facts about the Zeng	Size
—its size	—Zeng
—its horsepower	—Xanadu
—its initial cost	Horsepower
—its cost of maintenance	—Zeng
—its resale value	—Xanadu
Facts about the Xanadu	Initial cost
—its size	—Zeng
—its horsepower	—Xanadu
—its initial cost	Cost of maintenance
—its cost of maintenance	—Zeng
—its resale value	—Xanadu
	Resale value
	—Zeng
	—Xanadu

The plan you select depends upon your own needs and, in part, upon the amount of material you have to use. Generally, plan A is used for shorter assignments, where the reader is able to keep all of the facts closely connected. Plan B works better for longer assignments because it permits the reader constantly to see direct comparisons and contrasts between both cars.

Assume that the writer decided to use plan A for the paragraph on cars. The finished paragraph might look something like this:

After having studied all of the facts, I decided that in spite of its higher initial cost the Xanadu is a better car buy than its competitor, the Zeng. The Zeng is large and powerful—390 horses to pull it along. It sells for somewhere around $11,500 and its maintenance cost averages about $450 a year. However, it has a very low resale value. A year-old Zeng will bring in no more than $8,000. Apparently, no one wants a used Zeng. On the other hand, the Xanadu seems a far superior buy. It is about the same size as the Zeng, but it has a 440 horsepower motor. New, it sells for just under $13,500, but its yearly maintenance averages less than $200. And in regard to resale, the Xanadu depreciates only about $1000 a year. A five-year-old Xanadu is worth more than a two-year-old Zeng. So, it is really easy to see how much better a buy the Xanadu is.

topic sentence— key word is *facts*

Zeng Xanadu— transition phrase makes shift

Notice how the writer moves from one point to the other in the outline for plan A. Around the middle of the paragraph, the writer uses a transition phrase (*on the other hand*) to indicate a shift to the second broad category. She maintains unity by following the same outline point by point and by repeating the name of the first car in the second section.

Now, see how this paragraph might have been written according to plan B.

After having studied all of the facts, I decided that in spite of its higher initial cost, the Xanadu is a better buy than the Zeng. Both cars are the same size—barely room for two people. They have about the same power plants, although the Xanadu is fifty horses larger. A major difference is initial cost. The

topic sentence

size

horsepower

Zeng costs $11,500, and the Xanadu hits its buyer for about $13,500. The cost for service and parts is about the same for both cars. The real difference is in resale value. Apparently no one wants a used Zeng, but everyone seems to want a Xanadu no matter how old it is.

initial cost

maintenance cost

resale value

In both of these paragraphs, the writer could have included many more details. For example, she could have added sentences revealing the exact length of the cars, examples of maintenance costs, and exact figures for trade-in prices. The point is that whatever you choose to include should be organized according to a preconceived plan.

In thinking about the paragraph, the writer had to decide which to present first, the Zeng or the Xanadu. The choice was a typical one—order of importance. The case for the Xanadu, the writer's favorite, is strengthened by giving it the concluding position in the paragaph.

The first task in organizing a paragraph by comparison and contrast is to determine the list of items that you intend to use in your development. The following paragraph violates the important guideline that you must examine the same items for each of the objects that you are writing about.

Having tried the pizza at Raphael's and Tino's, I will now always go back to Raphael's for mine. The pizza at Raphael's has an unusually crisp crust and just the right amount of spice in the sauce. I usually get mushrooms and sausage for my topping, and Raphael's pizza comes with an abundant quantity of both. I don't really like Tino's anymore. Their pizza is expensive, and service is extremely slow. I once waited over an hour for my order to be filled. Tino's also has no atmosphere.

This paragraph is inadequately developed and possibly even unfair. It does not compare the same items at Raphael's and Tino's. Although the item-by-item comparison may have been clear in the writer's mind, it is not specific for the reader.

Exercise 17

The writer of this faulty paragraph could look at any of these items to make a valid comparison between Raphael's and Tino's: crust, sauce, toppings, price, service, and atmosphere. Develop a whole-by-whole (plan A) outline for an appropriately developed paragraph.

Exercise 18

Rearrange your material so it will conform to a part-by-part outline (plan B).

Exercise 19

Below are some sets of objects for comparison and contrast. For each set, indicate three to five items (categories for comparison and contrast) that you might use to develop a paragraph.

1. eating out and eating at home
2. watching television and going to a movie
3. living at home and living alone
4. writing a paper with a typewriter and writing a paper with a word processor
5. Two neighborhoods (cities, countries, etc.) in which you have lived

Exercise 20

Select the topic above that most interests you and develop a whole-by-whole outline.

Exercise 21

Now rearrange the same material so that it will conform to a part-by-part outline.

Exercise 22

Write a finished paragraph based on one of the outline schemes that you have just developed.

Below you are given scrambled information about two different department stores, Rosen's and Gilbert's. Which of these two stores would you prefer for your own shopping? Your response will depend upon your own personal interests, your economic situation, or any of several other items that reflect your individuality. Sort the meaningful information given below into categories that will lend themselves to a whole-by-whole scheme of organization. You might, for instance, group them under such headings as *types of merchandise*, *convenience*, and *special services*; but there are many other possibilities for your broad headings. You will not necessarily use all of the information given below, but you will use those specific things that support the categories you develop.

Develop an organizational scheme that will group your ideas into the whole-by-whole pattern of organization (say everything about Rosen's in the first half of your paragraph and everything about Gilbert's in the second half). Develop a finished paragraph based on your scheme. Don't forget to connect the parts of your paragraph with an appropriate transition.

Rosen's Department Store	**Gilbert's Department Store**
five floors of merchandise	accepts only MasterCard
accepts major credit cards	validates parking for two hours
very fashion oriented	petite and medium sizes emphasized
younger shoppers and clerks	charges for alterations
near the bus stop	huge bargain basement sales
mostly women's clothes	two large floors for shopping
large range of sizes	just off expressway
average to expensive prices	large selection of sports items
no alteration charge	conservative styles
emphasizes casual dress items	community dressing rooms
30-day lay-away plan	older shoppers and clerks
escalators and elevators	inexpensive to average prices
charge for gift wrapping	some alteration charges
charge for shopping bags	elevators but no escalators
merchandise grouped by designers	free shopping bags
private dressing rooms	free, simple gift wrapping
major seasonal sales	easy exchange policy

Rosen's Department Store	Gilbert's Department Store
rigid exchange policy	merchandise grouped by size
emphasizes bright colors	no lay-away plan
hair salon	some sale every month
small restaurant	large shoe selection
beauty consultants	blues, grays, and browns are main
open spaces, attractive displays	colors
taxi stand at door	small luncheon counter
many hats, scarves, and gloves	crowded, narrow aisles
inexpensive jewelry	bus stop two blocks away
carpeted floors	brand name coats and jackets
advertises frequently in newspapers	some Hispanic and Black clerks
mostly white clerks	wooden floors
a place to be seen shopping	advertises in windows of store only
	a place to find good bargains

Exercise 24

Let the ideas suggested in the previous exercise stimulate your thinking about two stores where you have frequently shopped. Develop your own list of specifics about the stores; organize that list and write a finished paragraph that compares and contrasts the two stores.

PROCESS ANALYSIS

Often you need to give someone directions for going to a certain place; sometimes you need to explain to someone how something works or how to make a particular item. Such a process of explanation is formally called *process analysis*. This is the type of development used to tell a new student how to find the campus bookstore, to explain how the filter screens on your home windows lower your heating bills, and to tell someone how to make a strawberry pie.

You must observe three fundamental principles in process analysis:

1. All necessary steps or reasons must be given.
2. Explanation should proceed in a systematic order structured by a time sequence.
3. Any unfamiliar terms must be defined or illustrated so that the reader will understand what is meant.

Obviously you have not told someone adequately how to bake your favorite cake if you have forgotten to mention that two eggs are added to the batter. An automobile manufacturer's directions on how to change a tire would be incomplete unless they included a reminder to block the automobile to keep it from rolling. All possible details must be included if the process is to be analyzed completely.

Furthermore, all details must be presented in the order in which they normally occur. If you are reading the owner's manual as you change your tire, you will not find a suggestion to block the car very helpful if it occurs in the last sentence of the directions. Nor would you find the notation to add two eggs to your cake very helpful if that reminder was made after you were told to bake the cake at 375 degrees for 45 minutes.

Similarly, any terms that the reader must understand in order to complete the process must be clearly explained. Sometimes this is done by a very brief definition; more often than not, it is accomplished through a brief physical description (manuals of direction often include actual pictures). If you are telling a newcomer to your city to turn left at the old Smythe building, you have not helped very much unless the building has a sign on it or unless you describe it so carefully that the newcomer will automatically know it upon sight. If you tell someone who is having difficulty unlocking a door to polish the key bit, you have not helped much if the individual does not know what a key bit is.

The structure for process analysis is really quite simple. The topic sentence usually states the task that is to be done and sometimes indicates the number of steps that will be required to complete the task. Each step in the process becomes a major support sentence and is followed by whatever details are necessary to make the description of that step in the process complete. A sample fencepost scheme looks like this:

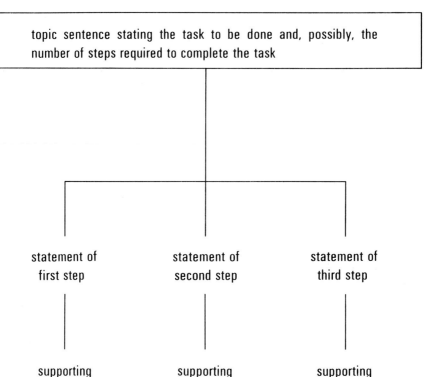

topic sentence stating the task to be done and, possibly, the number of steps required to complete the task

statement of first step

statement of second step

statement of third step

supporting details

supporting details

supporting details

If you have more than three steps, your structure obviously expands to make room for them. Transitional markers from one step to the next help emphasize the chronological nature of the process. Frequently they are as simple as *first, second,* or *third.* Sometimes they are words such as *next, after that, later, as soon as,* or *when that is done.*

Giving directions is a very common activity but one that not too many people do well. Too often directions are vague: "Go about three miles," "Turn left at either the second or third traffic light," or simply "You can't miss it." Good directions must be specific.

Exercise 25

Assume that you want to tell a new student how to go from your writing classroom to the registrar's office. Jot down answers to the following questions.

How many turns will the student have to make?

Which way will he or she turn each time?

Are there major markers—bulletin boards, stairs, drinking fountains, etc.—that can serve as visual guides along the way?

How will the student recognize the office when he or she gets there?

In this quick exercise, did you forget to tell the student which way to turn when he or she walked out of the classroom? Did you forget to tell on which side of the hallway the office was located? Compare your set of directions with those of your classmates.

Exercise 26

Select a location some distance from your campus, perhaps a post office, library, or church, and write a finished paragraph telling someone how to get there. You might first want to prepare a fencepost outline similar to the one on page 148. How many steps or turns must the individual make to reach the destination? Be careful to explain distances and locations specifically. If you mention a specific landmark, such as a store or specific house, at which the person is to turn, describe it briefly so it can be recognized. Use effective transition markers as you move from one step to the next.

When you are giving someone instructions for a particular activity, it is extremely important that those instructions be in chronological order. It is also important that you give the reason for any step in the process that your reader may question. Notice how one student explained her process for housebreaking a puppy:

Although it takes patience and personal availability, my own system for housebreaking a puppy works every time. The only equipment you need is a small kennel, which you can often borrow from the pet store where you bought the puppy, or a sturdy cardboard box. This kennel or box should be just large enough to let the puppy stand up or lie down, but it should not provide room for him to walk around. It is common knowledge that a healthy puppy will not foul its own sleeping quarters. Put the puppy in this temporary home the very first day, but carry him outside every hour. When he has relieved himself, bring him back inside, play with him a few minutes, and then put him back in his kennel. Continue this practice the second day, but now you should lift him out of the box, place him on the floor, and encourage him to follow you to the door. He will usually beat you. This step is important because it teaches him where the door to his outside world is. By the third day, you can extend the time between your trips outside to about two hours. Remember to play with him each time before putting him back in the kennel. Each successive day you lengthen the time between trips outside, but probably never any longer than four or five hours. After all, he is still just a puppy. The important thing is for him to know that you are there and that you will take him out. By the end of the first week, you should be able to leave him out of the kennel entirely, taking him outside at approximately the same time intervals you have been using. Watch, too, when he goes voluntarily to the door. That is his signal to you that he wants to go outside. Within two or three weeks you should be able to lengthen the time interval between trips outside so that the two of you make no more than two or three trips a day.

Exercise 27

One of the most confusing of all college activities is registration. Assume that you are writing a one-paragraph description of how to get through registration and that your instructions will be sent to the seniors in your former high school.

Where, exactly, do they go to register?

Whom do they ask for?

What items do they need to bring with them?

What forms must they complete?

Exercise 28

Arrange your material into an appropriate sequence of steps and write your finished paragraph. Be certain that your steps are arranged in time order and that you have provided enough details so that the reader can follow your instructions adequately.

Exercise 29

Imagine that you are writing a set of instructions for someone to follow. Select one of the following situations or plan a real one of your own.

instructions for a friend who is borrowing your car and you want him or her to know of some of its pecularities
instructions for a babysitter while you are out for the evening
instructions for someone who is going to feed your pets or water your plants while you are out of town
instructions for a student who is going to the library to try to find some information on the background of baseball's World Series

Remember that you will not be present while the task is being done. What does the individual need to know to complete the task? Think through the task carefully, arranging it into time sequences. Write your finished paragaph of instructions.

Select a rather complicated process to explain in your next paragraph. Some suggestions are given below, but you may wish to use an idea of your own.

adjusting the spark plug gap on your automobile
balancing the tone arm of your stereo
refinishing a favorite piece of furniture
formatting a disk for your computer

Since this task is somewhat technical, you need to think of terms that you might use in your instructions that will not be familiar to many readers. How can you define them so your reader will understand them? Write your finished paragraph, being careful to use enough details to make your instructions useful. Don't forget transitions as you move from one step in the process to the next.

CAUSAL ANALYSIS

In the previous section, you learned how to develop a paragraph that would explain how to do something. A related type of development is known as *causal analysis* and explains *why* something works the way it does. Causal analysis is therefore just what its name implies—a study of the *causes* that produce certain *effects*. Some texts refer to this type of development as *cause and effect development*.

When you write paragraphs of causal analysis, begin with a known fact—the effect. Develop your paragraph in a manner to show why the effect exists. For example, your effect might be that you were late to class this morning. In listing the causes, you should detail every actual reason for tardiness.

One of the temptations in writing causal analysis is to list only the most obvious causes—sometimes only one. Few effects have just *one* cause, although that may occasionally happen. Generally, numerous related causes are behind most effects.

You need not detail everything back to an absolute first cause. Such an effort would probably blame everything on poor Adam. But you must attempt to show *all relevant causes*. For example, if you are explaining why your doorbell rings when someone pushes the button, you do not need to become involved with explaining the whole process of electricity, which is obviously one of the causes, too.

A scheme for causal analysis begins with the topic sentence, a statement of the effect. Following this statement, you list the causes leading to the effect. Usually you list these in chronological order, but there may be times when you need to list them in order of increasing importance.

Here is a fencepost outline that one student used for his paragraph explaining why he was late for class:

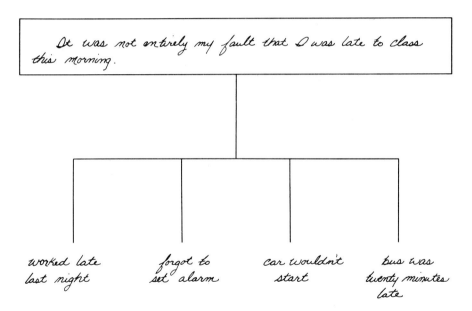

Notice that four causes are listed and that they are placed in chronological order. Each of these causes becomes a major support sentence in the student's finished paragraph. In the finished paragraph that follows, notice that the student does not present details for every cause. Some are so obvious that they do not require further explanation.

It was not entirely my fault that I was late to class this morning. Mr. Zoos kept me at work late   **topic sentence**

last night, and by the time I got home I was just too **first cause**
tired to remember to set the alarm. My muscles
ached from lifting boxes all evening; I could hardly **second cause**
wait to shower and get to bed. But I still would
have made it to school if only my car had started. **third cause**
My mother called me when I did not come down for
breakfast at the usual time. I jumped up, hurriedly
dressed, and dashed out to the car. The battery
was completely dead. I had been so tired the night
before that I had left the radio on. Mother drove me
the ten blocks to the bus stop and I waited, and
waited, and waited. Twenty minutes late, the bus **fourth cause**
finally got there. If I had not overslept, I would have
had time to walk to school, but as it was I arrived **conclusion**
nearly a half-hour late.

Although this student chose to develop his paragraph by arranging his causes in chronological order, you should remember that there are some times when you may wish to use the order of importance instead. If you were writing to analyze the causes of the pride that has just recently begun in your neighborhood, you would probably want to begin with the single most significant cause of that pride and then work backward in order of decreasing importance to examine other causes.

As you develop your causal analysis paragraphs in the following exercises, remember to include all of the important causes, to arrange them either in chronological order or by order of importance, and to add sufficient details to make your ideas interesting. Structure your paragraph so that the final sentence contains a restatement of the effect and serves as a summary to the entire paragaph. Remember, too, that in process analysis your emphasis is on *how*; in causal analysis your emphasis is on *why*.

Exercise 31

Select one of the following topics for your first causal analysis paragraph. Begin by thinking about the various causes that have led to the final effect. Will a discussion of those causes be more effective in chronological order or in order of importance? You might want to make yourself a fencepost outline (similar to the one on page 151) so that you can be certain that you have listed all of the important causes.

1. why you are going to college
2. why you have selected a particular major
3. why your neighborhood is an especially good (or bad) one
4. why the drug problem is so difficult to control
5. why compact discs are better than ordinary records

Exercise 32

For this paragraph, select some effect that seemed upsetting or tragic to you. You might use your own ideas for a topic, but here are some suggestions:

1. when you made a low or failing grade in a course
2. when you were severely scolded or fired from a job
3. when you broke up with a boyfriend/girlfriend or husband/wife
4. when you were stopped for a traffic violation

Since the topic you use for this assignment is one about which you have very strong feelings, be certain to sort them out before writing. What were the causes that led to the effect? How can you best arrange them to make your paragraph interesting?

Exercise 33

One problem with causal analysis is that people often have a hard time being objective about emotional issues. They tend to see everything from their own point of view. A major step in problem solving is to try to see a situation from another person's point of view.

Take the same topic you wrote about in Exercise 32, but this time analyze the effect from the point of view of the other person involved: your teacher, your boss, your boyfriend/girlfriend or husband/wife, the traffic officer, etc. Try to be objective. Think about what that other person would probably list as causes, not what you would list.

CAUSAL ANALYSIS AND PROBLEM SOLVING

Using causal analysis is the first step in problem solving. Before you can solve a problem, you must determine the exact causes of the problem. Two general patterns exist for structuring a piece of writing that both analyzes causes and offers solutions. In one you present the causes and follow each cause with your proposed solution(s). In the other you first present all of the causes and then present all of your proposed solutions. Typical fencepost outlines look something like this:

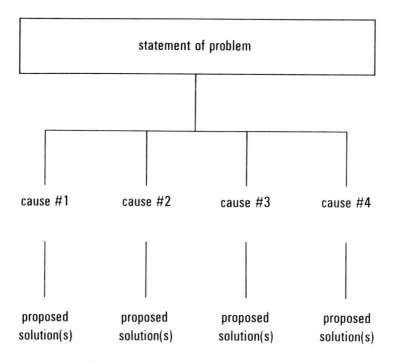

The writer who used the type of scheme on page 156 would present each cause and its proposed solution(s) separately.

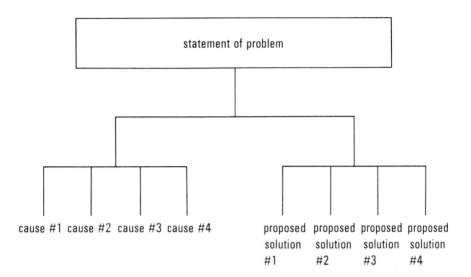

The writer who used the above type of scheme would first present all of the causes and then offer the proposed solutions.

Here is one student's paragraph analyzing causes and offering solutions for the lack of sufficient jobs for inexperienced workers during the summer months.

      If our city politicians are sincere about keeping the young people of the community meaningfully occupied next summer, they must begin to find job opportunities for the hundreds of young people who want to work but can't find jobs. Presently, too many potential employers say that they run a productive business and do not have the time or money to train inexperienced workers for short-term jobs. Other employers say that they have hired young workers before but have found them lazy and unreliable. And still other employers mention the

statement of problem

first cause

second cause

lack of a central job clearing house as a reason why they have hired so few young people for temporary jobs. While all of these are valid complaints, solutions must be found to remedy these problems and to provide the necessary jobs. For one thing, businesses that make their profits from the community should have a moral responsibility to put something, in this case jobs, back into that community. They should set up short training programs to prepare young workers for their summer jobs. And they should make sincere efforts to determine what skills these people have and to see if they can use the skills in their present workforce. Also, if they create proper motivational programs, the young workers will be much more enthusiastic about their work and will demonstrate better work habits. They must create appropriate meaningful jobs, not just counting paper clips and stacking delivery boxes, so these workers feel a part of the on-going progress of the company. They should create programs that reward excellence, that make the workers want to do their best. Finally, the city itself must structure a job clearing house to register all potential young workers and their interests and to maintain lists of all available jobs. There are even federal funds available to create these types of programs. High school and college advisors can become involved with job placement activities. The city might even host a job fair that would match workers with employers. It will certainly be less expensive in the long run to plan programs to make these young workers a part of the working community than it will be to provide detention facilities or public welfare. Attitudes toward work and work habits develop young, and our city must take aggressive steps now to turn what is a negative situation into a positive one.

third cause

transition to solutions

first solution

second solution

third solution

conclusion

Exercise 34

Write a finished paragraph in which you both analyze causes of a problem and offer proposed solutions. You might think of one of your own problems, but here are some suggestions:

1. getting financial assistance at your college
2. having a better relationship with your parents or other family member
3. developing a more friendly atmosphere in your neighborhood
4. correcting unfair procedures at your work or at school
5. redesigning a neighborhood park so it will be more useful to the residents

The Essay

From the Paragraph to the Essay

Illustration

Classification

Definition

Comparison and Contrast

Process Analysis

Causal Analysis

C H A P T E R

7 From the Paragraph to the Essay

The emphasis in this text has been on writing effective paragraphs. The reasons for this emphasis are valid ones. In many ways, the paragraph is a miniature essay. Now, you will quickly discover that many of the same techniques that you learned for writing paragraphs can also be used for writing essays. A paragraph has a *topic sentence* to announce its main idea; an essay has a *thesis sentence* or *statement* to do essentially the same task. Both the paragraph and the essay can be organized by using order of importance, order of time, or order of space. And both can be developed by following the general formulas for development that you studied in Chapter 6. If you have learned to write good paragraphs, you are well on your way toward writing good essays.

Like the paragraph, an essay develops one central idea. But the essay usually contains more details and offers more examples than does a typical paragraph. Dividing the different supporting ideas in your essay into separate paragraphs is one way to give each idea a distinct identity and thus an appropriate emphasis. If you wrote a five-page essay for one of your classes and wrote it all as one paragraph, it would be very difficult to read. There would be no breaks to guide the reader, no indentations to suggest that you were offering another example or moving to a different part of your topic.

As a matter of fact, some of the paragraph examples used previously in this text could also have been presented as short, multiparagraph essays. For now, remember that an essay has three essential parts: an introduction (a statement of your main idea, the thesis), a body (the development with examples or details of that main idea), and a conclusion (a summary of or an ending to what you have written). All of these parts are in the sample paragraph on page 79. Look at what happens to that paragraph if those parts are separated and written as several paragraphs.

I dislike those types of movies that do not deal with current, real-life situations. **thesis sentence**

Science fiction motion pictures are probably the ones I dislike the most. Movies with wildly conceived people, animals, or settings from some imaginary world turn me off. I would much rather see a scene set in Chicago or New York than in some unreal Planet X. And I prefer real human beings to robots and talking computers.

Running a close second on my "dislike list" are historic epics. Maybe I don't have enough background, but I find the retelling of past events boring. I have enough problems today without worrying about what happened in historic Greece or fifteenth-century England. **body paragraphs**

Sentimental love stories represent the third category of movies that I usually try to avoid. In real life everyone does not always get his woman or her man. Pretending that love is all pleasure and no pain sets up false standards for young people who have to live with real mates.

I guess I am just a hardheaded realist. **conclusion**

If the writer of these paragraphs wanted to add more detail, he or she probably could write about specific movies under each of the general categories. If this were done, the paragraphs would be quite long. In order to give emphasis to the different ideas, the writer might wish to use even more paragraph divisions. Look, for example, at the ideas presented in the first paragraph of the body. If the writer wanted to discuss specific movies, he or she might divide that one paragraph into separate paragraphs as follows:

a paragraph on science fiction movies with strange kinds of people
a paragraph on science fiction movies with obviously unreal animals
a paragraph on science fiction movies with wildly conceived settings.

The writer obviously could add additional examples and subdivide the other body paragraphs in a similar fashion.

Exercise 1

Several of the paragraph examples in Parts I and II of this text are long enough that they could actually be written as short, multiparagraph essays. Select either the example on pages 118–119 or pages 157–158 and by using the example above as a model, rewrite the original paragraph into an appropriate multiparagraph format.

Exercise 2

Select a paragraph that you wrote for an earlier exercise in this text and rewrite it into a multiparagraph format.

WRITING THE INTRODUCTION TO AN ESSAY

When you were writing paragraphs, you typically began with your *topic statement*, a one-sentence statement of what you intended to write about. The similar sentence that announces and limits the topic of an essay is called the *thesis sentence* or *thesis statement*. Since a thesis sentence works with the essay in the same way that the topic sentence works with the paragraph, you might wish to review the guidelines discussed on pages 64–66 for writing good topic sentences. Those same guidelines will help you to write good thesis sentences as well.

The introduction to an essay, however, is usually more than the one sentence statement of thesis. In addition to announcing your topic, the introduction should also get your reader's attention. Think briefly about your own attitudes as a reader. How many times have you read the first few sentences of a magazine article and then quit because they failed to get your attention? And how many times have you glanced quickly at another article without intending to read it and found yourself halfway through reading it before you realized what you were doing? When this has happened to you, you have usually been caught by the attention device in the introduction.

Think, then, of an introduction as having two basic parts: a thesis statement and an attention device. The attention device, quite simply, is anything that you can use to get your reader's attention, to pull your readers inside your essay. Some of the most frequently used attention devices make use of a brief narrative, statistics, quotations, shocking statements, or rhetorical questions. The type of attention device that you use in a given situation depends on your topic and your audience.

Here is a set of sample introductions for each of the attention devices mentioned above. Notice how each ends with a thesis statement.

Narrative Introduction

The most frequently used attention device is the narrative. Almost everyone likes to hear a story, so one of the best ways to get your reader's attention is to tell them a story. Think of a personal experience that will let you lead naturally into your topic.

Even today I find it somewhat sad to think that the one thing I most often recall about Uncle Ernest was not the most important thing about him. Actually, Uncle Ernest was my mother's uncle, and the thing I most often remember about him was that he could not read or write. I don't often remember about his raising four children alone after his first wife died, and I don't think much about the summer I spent with him when he taught me how to fish. I just remember that he could not read or write and that I felt sorry for him. When he was courting the woman who later became his second wife, he used to bring her love letters over to our house for Mother to read to him. When I was in the eighth grade, he would stop by our house every afternoon for me to read the newspaper to him. As young as I was, I learned a very important lesson from Uncle Ernest. Reading and writing are such important skills that no one must be allowed to grow up without them.

Statistical Introduction

For some topics, you can arrest your readers' attention by first presenting them with an important set of statistics.

According to a report that we just read in my sociology class, fifteen million adult Americans cannot read or write at all and another twenty-seven million cannot read or write well enough to address an envelope or complete an ordinary job application form by themselves. Seventy-six percent of this total group are receiving some form of welfare payments from the government. Specialists say that their lack of basic reading and writing skills will keep most of these people among America's unemployed for their entire lives. Reading and writing are such important skills that no one must be allowed to grow up without them.

Quotation Introduction

Often you can get your readers' attention by beginning your essay with a quotation. You must be careful, though, that you don't force the quotation upon your topic. A quotation will work more effectively if your readers know that your source is an authority on your topic. Although your cousin Suzanne Golub may have said something very striking about reading and writing skills, a quotation from her would not be effective for readers who do not know her unless, for instance, you can also explain that she is an English teacher at a recognized college.

Almost in jest Benjamin Franklin wrote, "If you would not be forgotten, as soon as you are dead and rotten, either write things worth reading, or do things worth writing." What Franklin didn't say was that if there is no one to do the writing and no one to do the reading you will still be forgotten "as soon as you are dead and rotten." Our civilization depends upon writers and readers to keep its records. Schools must move the teaching of reading and writing to the top of their priority list.

Startling Introduction

Sometimes the best way to get your readers' attention is to startle them, to shock them. Often you can use a very shocking, even controversial, idea at the beginning of an essay to jolt your readers to attention.

People who cannot read or write deserve no sympathy from the rest of us. We should stop trying to help these kinds of people and devote our resources to the real producers in our society. Although not very many people actually express these thoughts, they seem to be the philosophy by which a large portion of our society lives. But this philosophy is wrong, and we cannot ignore these individuals any longer. Reading and writing are such important skills that everyone should have the opportunity to learn them.

Rhetorical Questions

Rhetorical questions (those questions that we ask but do not expect to be answered) are frequently effective ways to begin an essay because they let you address your readers directly. If you begin your introduction with a series of rhetorical questions in a carefully written parallel pattern, you create a sentence rhythm that automatically pulls your reader into your essay.

Can you imagine how your life would be if you could not read? Can you imagine how your life would be if you could not write? Can you imagine how your life would be if you could help others learn to read and write? One of the first steps is coming to an awareness that there are dozens of people in this community who want to read and write and who need help. With the right attitude, you may be the most important person who can teach them these vital skills of communication.

Exercise 3

Select one of the paragraphs that you wrote for a previous assignment. Using the general types of introductions you have learned, write at least two different paragraph-long introductions for your original paragraph. Include both a thesis sentence and an attention device.

Select the one paragraph-long introduction that you feel works best with your original paragraph and write a two-paragraph essay: your new introduction and your original paragraph. Remember that you may have to edit or delete the topic sentence in that original paragraph to keep from repeating ideas that are now in your introduction.

DEVELOPING THE BODY OF AN ESSAY

The way you develop the body of your essay will depend upon the topic about which you are writing and upon the purpose of your writing. In Chapter 6 you studied six different types of development: illustration, classification, definition, comparison and contrast, process analysis, and causal analysis. The six types of development, sometimes called *modes of discourse* or *rhetorical modes*, are among the most useful means of developing ideas in your essays. Each of these six modes will be examined in a separate chapter to help you work with them in multiparagraph writing.

As you study these modes, remember that there is nothing mysterious or magical about them. Each of them is really a way of thinking that you use everyday. As you use them in your writing, you are taking a rather natural system of thinking with which you are subconsciously familiar and consciously applying it to your writing.

DEVELOPING THE CONCLUSION OF AN ESSAY

Ending your essay effectively is just as important as beginning it effectively. Don't drag out your conclusion; for most of the essays that you write in college, a one-paragraph conclusion is sufficient. Sometimes even a one-sentence conclusion works effectively. Remember the times you have listened to speakers who said they were concluding their talks but who continued for another ten or fifteen mintues. When you are ready to end, end.

Make your conclusion read like a real conclusion. Your readers should know from the first words that you are finishing your essay, and they should not have to know this from your use of a label such as "In conclusion...." You can use other more effective transitional words and phrases, and sometimes you can most effectively conclude by referring to your entire essay. Your conclusion might begin with phrases like these:

When I reflect upon these experiences, I realize....
It is quite clear, then, that an educated public will....
Based upon all of this evidence, an educated person has to recognize that....
Finally, it is quite evident that....
After thinking about all of these ideas, you must admit that you have little choice but to....

An old piece of advice for communicators, both speakers and writers, is to *tell your audience what you are going to do* (your introduction), *do it* (your body), and *tell them what you have done* (your conclusion). An effective conclusion should summarize the major ideas from the body of your essay without restating them. Sometimes your conclusion may be nothing more than a careful rewording of your thesis sentence.

You will often find an effective conclusion to be one that repeats a pattern you used in the introduction. That is, if you began your essay with a narrative introduction, return to a major idea in that narrative for your conclusion. If you started your essay with a set of dramatic statistics, refer to those statistics again as you end your essay.

Notice how these sample conclusions "borrow from" the introductions:

I know that I will never forget Uncle Ernest and how his inability to read and write affected me. Now that I am a college student and have had experience tutoring in our neighborhood learning center, I know there is only one career for me. I must be a teacher, and I must teach people like my Uncle Ernest to read and write.

These statistics shout to us all, offering striking evidence that Americans can no longer sit idly by while nearly fifty million of our neighbors lack the reading and writing skills necessary to function in our society. For much too long now, we have swept most of these people under the welfare rug and pretended that they did not exist. But we can no longer take this escapist position. We must come to terms with teaching vital reading and writing skills to everyone.

Exercise 5

Reread the two introductions that you wrote for Exercise 3. Now write two different conclusions, letting each of them borrow from the ideas in your introduction.

Exercise 6

Select the conclusion you feel works best with the two-paragraph essay that you wrote for Exercise 4. Write a three-paragraph essay that includes a paragraph for your introduction, a paragraph for the body, and a paragraph for your conclusion.

8

Illustration

In the paragraph section of this text, you learned that one of the most effective ways to develop your ideas was through illustration. With this system, you use one or more examples to illustrate the point that you are making. *For a review of the basic organizational principles of illustration, you might want to reread pages 112–116.*

AN ILLUSTRATION ESSAY

Here are the rough draft and final copy of Susan's illustration essay. Read both of them carefully so you can respond to the discussion questions that follow.

My husband and I attended our yearly "Krissmörgie" party ~~this~~ *last*

~~past~~ Saturday evening. Krissmörgie is a combination of words that

means "Christmas smorgasbord" in Swedish. ~~This~~ *Our* first Christmas

smorgasbord was held ten years ago, when all ~~the invited~~ couples *of those* *attending* were ∧

members of the same church. It is interesting to reflect∧on how the party *both*

and the people who attend∧have changed through the years.

The first party was a gala affair. We had hand~~made~~ *printed* invitations and

∧tickets ~~with numbers on them~~ for a door prize drawing. We paid $12 a *numbered* couple so ~~to have~~ several of us *Could* form a committee and do all the

shopping and preparing of the food. ~~In recent years,~~ *Now* invitations ~~have~~

~~been~~ *made* by telephone. The cost of a ticket is ~~now~~ $2.50 a person to cover *only*

the cost of paper goods and beverages, and everyone brings an item of

food for the table. ~~No one goes~~ *None of the women* out to buy a new dress anymore, but

wears comfortable skirts or slacks. The men no longer wear suits and

ties, but come dressed in sweaters and turtlenecks.

In the ten years we have met, there have been other, deeper

changes. Our church went through a very traumatic split five years ago,

and now, instead of seeing each other at least once a week, we attend

five different churches and some of us see each other only once a year

~~now,~~ at our Chriasmas gathering. Through the years ~~engaged couples~~

~~have~~ those who were single have brought their dates, gotten married,

and had children. We have also had two divorces in the group. Last year,

Nancy and Van did not come to the Krissmörgie, after divorcing several

months earlier. This year both were there, although they maintained

their distances throughout the evening by making sure they were in

separate rooms as much as possible. David brought his new girlfriend

this year. At this point, *though* it is hard to include an outsider in a group that

has remained constant for so long. *In the ten years,* Some couples have had babies, some

have become "empty-nesters," and are enjoying the freedom to travel,

and one couple has grandchildren.

The years seem to be taking their toll in some ways. Our first parties lasted well into the night; this year everyone was ready to leave by 11:30 pm. In the early years we would play charades or divide into groups to sing Christmas carols as baa-ing sheep, quacking ducks, or mooing cows. This year everyone voted to forego the games. One tradition that we do carry on is the exchange of a white elephant gift. Through the years we have collected two gifts that are recycled every year—a bunch of ragged-looking crocheted carrots, and a man's cotton red vest. The yearly challenge is to wrap these two items in a clever way, so people will never suspect they are selecting these treasured, but dreaded white elephants. We enjoyed a good laugh this year, as a lucky husband and wife were the recipients of both of these wonderful gifts. Saturday evening saw the addition of another white elephant destined to be passed on year after year—a pair of XXX large men's boxer shorts!

Since many of us now see each other only once a year, our conversations have dipped to a very superficial level. Once we have asked how the children are and what everyone is doing as far as work, the conversations tend to die, and we move on to someone else. The relationships have not been nurtured throughout the year, and there is little to feed on to keep a conversation going.

Driving home, my husband and I discuss how much weight many of the women have put on, how gray or balding some of the men have gotten, and our own personal opinions of an individual comment we heard. Of course, every other couple is probably doing the same thing— only ~~this~~ *when they talk* time Neil and I are the couple being mentioned as the one that has changed.

As little as we have in common with many of the other couples, I'm sure we will continue ~~to look forward to our next years~~ *yearly* get-togethers. Kay and Stefen have ✓volunteered their home for next ~~December~~ *year's party*. I imagine Karen and Pat drove home discussing how they would ~~camo-~~ *Camouflage* ~~flogue~~ the infamous carrots, ~~and~~ vest, *and boxer shorts* for the next unsuspecting gift selector. Although situations *and* & people change, traditions are hard to change, especially at Christmas.

My husband and I attended our yearly "Krissmörgie" party last Saturday evening. Krissmörgie is a combination of words that means "Christmas smorgasbörd" in Swedish. Our first Christmas smorgasbörd was held ten years ago, when all of those couples attending were members of the same church. It is interesting to reflect both on how the party and the people who attended have changed through the years.

The first party was a gala affair. We had handprinted invitations and numbered tickets for a door prize drawing. We paid $12 a couple so several of us could form a committee and do all the shopping and preparing of the food. Now, invitations are made by telephone. The cost of a ticket is $2.50 a person to cover only the cost of paper goods and beverages, and everyone brings an item of food for the table. None of the women go out to buy a new dress anymore, but wear comfortable skirts or slacks. The men no longer wear suits and ties, but come dressed in sweaters and turtlenecks.

In the ten years we have met, there have been other, deeper changes. Five years ago, our church went through a very traumatic split and now, instead of seeing each other at least once a week, we attend five different churches and some of us see each other only once a year, at our Christmas gathering. Through the years those who were single have brought their dates, gotten married, and had children. We have also had two divorces in the group. Last year, Nancy and Van did not come to the Krissmörgie, after divorcing several months earlier. This year both were there, although they maintained their distances throughout the evening by making sure they were in separate rooms as much as possible. David brought his new girlfriend this year. At this point, though, it is hard to include an outsider in a group that has remained constant for so long. In the ten years, some couples have had babies, some have become "empty-nesters," and are enjoying the freedom of travel, and one couple has grandchildren.

The years seem to be taking their toll in some ways. Our first parties lasted well into the night. This year everyone was ready to leave by 11:30 pm. In the early years we would play charades or divide into groups to sing Christmas carols as baa-ing sheep, quacking ducks, or mooing cows. This year everyone voted to forego the games.

One tradition that we do carry on is the exchange of a white elephant gift. Through the years we have collected two gifts that are recycled every year—a bunch of ragged-looking crocheted carrots, and a man's red cotton vest. The yearly challenge is to wrap these two items in a clever way, so people will never suspect they are selecting these treasured but dreaded white elephants. We enjoyed a good laugh this year, as a lucky husband and wife were the recipients of both of these wonderful gifts. Saturday evening saw the addition of another white elephant destined to be passed on year after year—a pair of XXX large men's boxer shorts!

Since many of us now see each other only once a year, our conversations have dipped to a very superficial level. Once we have asked how the children are and what everyone is doing as far as work, the conversations tend to die, and we move on to someone else. The relationships have not been nurtured throughout the year, and there is little to feed on to keep a conversation going.

Driving home, my husband and I discuss how much weight many of the women have put on, how gray or balding some of the men have gotten, and our own personal opinions of an individual comment we heard. Of course, every other couple is probably doing the same thing—only when they talk Neil and I are the couple being mentioned as the one that has changed.

As little as we have in common with many of the other couples, I'm sure we will continue our yearly get-togethers. Kay and Stefen have volunteered their home for next year's party. I imagine Karen and Pat drove home discussing how they would camouflage the infamous carrots, vest, and boxer shorts for the next unsuspecting gift selector. Although situations and people change, traditions are hard to change, especially at Christmas.

For Discussion

1. What kinds of changes did Susan make from her rough draft to her final copy? In what ways do the changes help to make the final copy better?
2. Which sentence in the first paragraph is the thesis sentence?
3. What transition signals does Susan use at the beginning of the six paragraphs that make up the body of her essay?
4. What makes the conclusion to this essay effective? How does it work to reflect on the thesis sentence of the first paragraph?

WRITING YOUR OWN ILLUSTRATION ESSAY

An effective way to organize your own essay is to use an introductory paragraph that contains your thesis sentence and a reference to the separate incidents that you will describe. Follow this paragraph with a carefully constructed paragraph for each separate incident, being certain to tie all parts together with effective transition signals. You might end your short essay with a brief concluding paragraph in which you pull together your various incidents and relate them once more to your thesis sentence. A working model for such an essay might be something like this:

I have seen so much hypocrisy that I have trouble believing anyone anymore. This hypocrisy seems to be everywhere. I have seen it in my parents, my minister, and my classmates.	**introduction: thesis sentence and indication of parts of essay**

My parents show their hypocrisy when we talk about the drug versus alcohol issue. (follow with specific illustration)

My minister argues for simple living, but he drives a $25,000 car. (follow with specific illustration)

Finally, my classmates are hypocritical in their reasons for going to college. (follow with specific illustration)

If I can't trust my parents, my minister, or my classmates, I just don't think that I can believe anyone.

one body paragraph

a second body paragraph

a third body paragraph

concluding paragraph

Exercise

Here are some broad topics for your consideration. Select one of these, and, using an organization scheme similar to the one above, develop it into an essay that is four or five paragraphs long.

the way your family celebrates a particular holiday
the most exciting (or the most depressing) day in your life
problems with being a parent and going to college
problems with working and going to college
why social snobs miss so much fun in life

C H A P T E R

9

Classification

If you have enough details for each of your classes (categories, types, or kinds), your writing will be more readily understood if you develop it as a multiparagraph essay rather than as one very long paragraph. Remember that your major task is to show the relationship of the various classes to the whole, the complete topic that you identify in your thesis sentence. *For a review of the basic organizational principles of classification, you might want to reread pages 120–124.*

A CLASSIFICATION ESSAY

Maryellyn works at a weight loss organization that calls itself TOPS, Take Off Pounds Sensibly. Her experience at this job gave her the opportunity to observe the different people in the program and to classify them into three distinct divisions. Here are her rough draft and final version of that classification.

> Each Monday evening I am faced with the challenge of trying to convince eighty-four overweight people to take responsibility for their own eating habits.

> Since there are so many different people in the TOPS (Take off Pounds Sensibly) program, I find it interesting to put them into groups according to their attitudes.

~~There are three different types of TOPS (Take Off Pounds Sensibly) members in our chapter.~~ I like to call them Losers ③, Turtles ②, and Socializers ①.

The Socializers are ~~a fun~~ *an elite* group. ~~Their main concern is to~~ *They only* pay their dues so ~~they have~~ *they'll* ~~can come every week and~~ *somewhere to* party *every week* ~~These people~~ *They consistantly gain weight,* sit in the back rows, and tell jokes and funny stories from the time they finish weighing in—with another gain—until I turn off the lights and send them ~~back home~~ *on their way*. They ~~don't~~ seem to be ~~aware~~ *unaware* of the ~~rest of~~ *other members of* the group and I wonder if they would even know ~~any of~~ the other members ~~by~~ *what TOPS stands for.* ~~name if they met them on the street.~~

The largest group consists of ~~On the other hand,~~ the Turtles, who are *also* the most negative ~~members~~ *people* I have ever dealt with. These chronic complainers can turn a simple ~~suggestion~~ *comment* into a major controversy. They ~~seem to feed on~~ *create* (by interrupting the speaker and getting off the subject) ~~creating~~ a disturbance during the program ~~and to feed~~ *thrive* on each other's *the most popular of which are these:* feeble excuses, ~~These are some of the most popular~~ " I'm holding water,

I'm allergic to most vegetables, I had to go to a wedding," "it's the medicine I'm taking," "it's my husband's birthday," and "there must be something wrong with the scale." It is not uncommon for ~~Turtles~~ them to lose a pound one week only to gain it back the next week, and thus the name Turtles. The scale never seems to move for them from one year to the next.

However, the members who take advantage of TOPS as a weight loss organization, I accurately call Losers. I can always ~~count~~ depend on a Loser to contribute constructively to each meeting, and they instinctively give emotional support to members who need it. ~~and their weight chars reflect their positive attitude.~~ Since they earn prizes for their successes, as well as a slimmer ~~figure~~ their figures, smiles can ~~usually~~ always be found on ~~a Loser's face. These members'~~ their faces. The Loser's hands ~~can usually~~ are the first to be ~~raised~~ offered when a call is made for volunteers to ~~do a~~ form a committee or to help ~~on~~ with a special projects.

When I ~~turn over~~ retire my gavel ~~at the end of my term~~ next April, it will not be difficult for me to know which group I'll ~~be in.~~ join. I'm sure The Socializers ~~probably~~ won't want me; ~~would not let me in,~~ the Turtles ~~wouldn't~~ won't like me; but the Losers ~~would~~ will welcome me with open arms.

The Losers Are Winners

Each Monday evening I am faced with the challenge of trying to convince eighty-four overweight people to take responsibility for their own eating habits. Since there are so many different people in the TOPS (Take Off Pounds Sensibly) program, I find it interesting to put them into groups according to their attitudes. I like to call them Socializers, Turtles, and Losers.

The Socializers are an elite group. They only pay their dues so they'll have somewhere to party every week. They consistently gain weight, sit in the back rows, and tell jokes and funny stories from the time they finish weighing in—with another gain—until I turn off the lights and send them on their way. They seem unaware of the other members of the group and I wonder if they even know what TOPS stands for.

The largest group consists of the Turtles, who are also the most negative people I have ever dealt with. These chronic complainers can turn a simple comment into a major controversy. They create a disturbance during the program by interrupting the speaker and getting off the subject, and they thrive on each other's feeble excuses, the most popular of which are these: "I'm holding water," "I'm allergic to most vegetables," "I had to go to a wedding," "it's the medicine I'm taking," "it's my husband's birthday," and "there must be something wrong with the scale." It is not uncommon for them to lose a pound one week only to gain it back the next week, and thus the name Turtles. The scale never seems to move for them from one year to the next.

However, the members who take advantage of TOPS as a weight loss organization, I accurately call Losers. I can always depend on a Loser to contribute constructively to each meeting, and they instinctively give emotional support to members who need it. Since they earn prizes for their successes, as well as their slimmer figures, smiles can usually be found on their faces. A Loser's hands are the first to be raised when a call is made for volunteers to form a committee or to help with a special project.

When I retire my gavel next April, it will not be difficult for me to know which group I'll join. I'm sure the Socializers probably won't want me; the Turtles won't like me; but the Losers will welcome me with open arms.

For Discussion

1. Maryellyn's rough draft has no title, but her finished essay does. How does this title work with the major ideas of her essay?

2. Look at the second sentence of Maryellyn's rough draft and see how she has renumbered her three classes into a different order than she used in her final essay. What principle does she use for this new sequence?

3. What words does the author use in each of the paragraphs of the body of her essay to remind her reader that the class she is writing about is also a part of a larger group (in this case the complete TOPS membership)?

4. How do you know from just the first sentence of Maryellyn's conclusion that this is to be the final paragraph of her essay?

WRITING YOUR OWN CLASSIFICATION ESSAY

When you write your own multiparagraph classification essay, list in your introduction the names (labels) of the classes or categories that you intend to examine, being certain to name them in the same order that you will write about them in your paper. You then treat each separate class in a new paragraph, and you summarize all of your classes in a brief conclusion. A model for this type of system might look something like this:

Yes, I would love prime rib every night. Yes, I crave about five pounds of smoked salmon. And, yes, I get excited just thinking about escargot. But the simple truth is that I'm a student on a student's budget, and these wonderful foods come along for special occasions only. For the rest of the time, I get to select from the more usual food that a college student can afford: hamburgers, pizza, and hot dogs.

Introductory paragraph includes attention device, thesis sentence, and a listing of the three foods to be discussed in the essay.

When I have my choice among the different kinds of inexpensive food, I definitely pick hamburgers. (follow with supporting details)

My second favorite student-type food is pizza. (follow with supporting details)

Sometimes I even resort to eating the lowly hot dog. (follow with supporting details

The body paragraphs are arranged by order of importance.

I suppose that as long as I am a student on a tight budget I will have to continue filling myself with hamburgers, pizza, and, when absolutely necessary, hot dogs.

The conclusion refers again to all three kinds of food and makes a summary evaluation.

Exercise

Select one topic from those suggested below and develop it into a multiparagraph essay. Remember to make your divisions of classification with a specific audience and purpose (see pages 125–127) in mind.

kinds of people with whom you work (or socialize)
types of television commercials
moral attitudes among college students
kinds of people who shape the lives of others

C H A P T E R

10

Definition

The multiparagraph essay of definition, sometimes called the extended definition, usually does two things. It defines a term by showing how it is different from similar terms with which it might be confused. Then it emphasizes the significance of those differences by giving extended illustrations or examples. After reading these extended illustrations, the reader knows quite clearly what makes this particular term different from similar terms. *For a review of the basic organizational principles for definition, you might want to reread pages 131–134.*

A DEFINITION ESSAY

The rough draft that is printed below is what Valerie originally wrote for the definition essay. For this draft, she was interested in working out the dictionary meaning of her term in English and with showing how the particular kind of time she was defining was unique.

Carefully read Valerie's rough draft and then the final version of her definition essay.

Gemütlichkeit is a Germanic expression ~~used to~~ refer*s* _that_ to a very

special time spent enjoying the close and yet informal company of

others. The word is roughly translated from the Middle English

felawschip, which later became fellowship. In the German ~~language it~~ *word*
comes from ~~the word~~ gemütlich, meaning comfortable or snug. When the
suffix <u>keit</u> is added, the word becomes a noun meaning comfortableness
or kindliness. ~~It is used~~ in Germany ~~to~~ *it* refer *s* to a social gathering of
friends who expressly enjoy each others company. Throughout the
country sides of West Germany this type of ~~fellowship and socializing~~ *social gathering* is
commonplace.

The ~~kirke~~ (church) plays its role *in gemütlichkeit* by placing emphasis on togetherness and sharing. People ~~and families~~ come together *on the church grounds* and share common
interests with their friends and neighbors ~~of the congregation~~. Men and
women huddle in their various groups to exchange news while their
children play about the ~~church grounds~~ *lawn*. It is a time for sharing and
enjoying, not one for being serious. ~~This old German custom was carred~~
~~over with the Pennsylvania Dutch, ending up in the German Protestant~~
~~church. Today~~ many *German* churches still have a fellowship hour that's usually
held prior to the late morning service.

<u>Gemütlichkeit</u> can also be found in any beer hall in West Germany.
Village
~~Towns~~ people gather in the early evening to socialize while enjoying
music and beer. In fact, the socializing is usually more important than
the music or the beer. It is a fun time when people have no other
(purpose) than to enjoy each other's company. While everyone joins in
singing the boisterous beer songs, ~~there is a lot of~~ *they also enjoy* good natured

laughing, slapping on the back, and story telling. It is, indeed, a snug time among friends who enjoy themselves and ~~enjoy~~ each other.

This German <u>gemütlichkeit</u> is unlike the typical social scene in America. Here people are still too concerned about their image, too aware of their own presence. Very few Americans would think about gathering an hour before their church service just to relax, swap stories, and share laughs with close friends. And the German beer hall will never be replaced in its spirit of gemutlichkeit with the stuffy American cocktail hour or with the ~~tense~~ *frantic* scene at its singles bars.

Sometimes I think Americans just don't know how to relax.
∧ ~~This type of night life is so much less formal than ours.~~ Even though ~~our people~~ *we* take pride in being "open," we're actually a very private, guarded, and self-centered lot. The warmth and basic lack of trust towards our fellow man has been lost. The days of simply letting go and enjoying ourselves in an unstructured social setting are gone.

Maybe we need to reinvent what the Germans invented centuries ago: the gemütlichkeit.

move to introduction

Sometimes I think Americans just don't know how to relax. Even though we take pride in being "open," we're actually a very private, guarded, and self-centered lot. The warmth and basic lack of trust towards your neighbor has been lost. The days of simply letting go and enjoying ourselves in an unstructured social setting are gone. Maybe we need to reinvent what the Germans invented centuries ago: the gemütlichkeit.

Gemütlichkeit is a Germanic expression that refers to a very special time spent enjoying the close and yet informal company of others. The word is roughly translated from the Middle English *felawschip*, which later became *fellowship*. The German word comes from gemütlich, meaning comfortable or snug. When the suffix *keit* is added, the word becomes a noun meaning comfortableness or kindliness. In Germany it refers to a social gathering of friends who expressly enjoy each other's company. Throughout the countryside of West Germany this type of social gathering is commonplace.

The church plays its role in gemütlichkeit by placing emphasis on togetherness and sharing. People come together on the church grounds and share common interests with their friends and neighbors. Men and women huddle in their various groups to exchange news while their children play about the church lawn. It is a time for sharing and enjoying, not one for being serious. Many churches in Germany still have a fellowship hour that's usually held prior to the late morning service.

Gemütlichkeit can also be found in any beer hall in West Germany. Village people gather in the early evening to socialize while enjoying music and beer. In fact, the socializing is usually more important than the music or the beer. It is a fun time when people have no purpose other than to enjoy each other's company. While everyone joins in singing the boisterous beer songs, they also enjoy good natured laughing, slapping on the back, and story telling. It is, indeed, a snug time among friends who enjoy themselves and enjoy each other.

This German gemütlichkeit is unlike the typical social scene in America. Here people are still too concerned about their image, too aware of their own presence. Very few Americans would think about gathering an hour before their church service just to relax, swap stories, and share laughs with close friends. And the German beer hall will never be replaced in its spirit of gemütlichkeit with the stuffy American cocktail hour or with the frantic scene at its singles bars.

For Discussion

1. Notice that the final paragraph of Valerie's rough draft has been revised somewhat and is now used as her introduction. How effective is this introduction at setting up the topic for her paper?

2. Valerie spends a part of her time tracing the meaning of gemütlichkeit back to its Middle English and German origins. Do these references help make her subsequent discussion of the word more effective?
3. What are the various "parts" of Valerie's essay? How does she bring all of these parts together in her conclusion?

WRITING YOUR OWN DEFINITION ESSAY

Exercise 1

A problem that readers sometimes have is that they do not read a particular word and think the same meaning that you intended. Different words suggest different meanings to various people in various circumstances.

Select one word from the list below and define it in *all* of the contexts given. Each context will require one or more paragraphs of development. Remember that within each context you must work within the word-class-differences framework, and also that you must include appropriate minor levels of support to make your definition interesting and meaningful.

word	context
heavy	used by someone carrying a large package
	used casually by someone to describe an idea
rake	used by a farmer to describe one of his or her tools
	used by a beautician to describe an instrument for grooming the hair
	used by a novelist to describe a type of person
gay	used to describe a general feeling
	used to describe a life-style

word	context
light	used to contrast with darkness
	used by someone carrying a package
	used by a beer manufacturer
slip	used to describe something one wears
	used to describe an extremely narrow object
	used to describe an error in thinking

You will want to organize your essay so that the reader knows from the first paragraph that you are going to talk about several meanings of the word. A valid organization pattern might be something like this:

Often it is important that you know something about the writer and the intended audience in order to get the correct meaning from a specific word. For instance, the word *proof* would not mean the same thing when used by or for a lawyer, a printer, and a brewmaster. **introduction**

If a lawyer uses the word, he or she means a form of evidence acceptable in the courtroom. (follow with details of development)

If a printer uses the word, he or she is referring to a trial sheet of copy. (follow with **body paragraphs** details of development)

A brewmaster who talks about *proof* is making reference to the alcoholic strength of his or her product. (follow with details of development)

Knowing who is writing and to whom is **conclusion** obviously important. Otherwise you might confuse signed testimony with a galley or, worse yet, with a pint of ale.

Exercise 2

Develop your own extended definition of one of the following words or terms:

substance abuse
computer hacking
identity crisis
marriage
good citizen
academic ability

C H A P T E R

11 Comparison and Contrast

Stop for a moment and think how often throughout a typical day you make comparisons and contrasts. Everytime you make a judgment about two or more persons or things, you are comparing and contrasting. You do this when you decide whether you want to spend the afternoon with Anthony or Julio, and you do it when you decide whether you want to buy a red scarf or a blue one. Throughout your day, you make dozens of judgments based on informal comparisons and contrasts. In this chapter you are asked to let that same system of thinking structure your writing. *For a review of the basic organizational principles of comparison and contrast, you might want to reread pages 138–141.*

A COMPARISON AND CONTRAST ESSAY

When Maryellyn wrote the rough draft that appears below, she tentatively titled her work "The Challenge of Writing." Later she revised her rough draft and rewrote it with a new title: "Writing for Myself or Others." Carefully read both drafts to see what Maryellyn did in her revision to give greater emphasis to the formula for comparison and contrast writing.

The Challenge of Writing

I've enjoyed writing all my life, but

~~Ever~~ since I began this ~~college~~ composition class, I've had ~~trouble~~ *much difficulty*

putting my pen to paper.

^writing. It was much easier writing only for myself, because then I did

not have to worry about using proper grammar *or an effective style* for someone else's

benefit. Before I took this course, I would write only for me. My ~~only~~

to capture private thoughts and feelings.

concern was, ~~for my thoughts about what I was going through or how I~~

~~felt about things.~~ I would take my pen in hand, get some paper, and

write. The pen in my hand would ~~move~~ *glide* across the page *leaving a* ~~telling about my~~

message from my soul.

~~various thoughts~~. The time passed quickly and the pages ~~were~~ filled fast.

felt an attraction to the

I always ~~liked the~~ empty page. I was never at a loss for words.

A sense of kinship and closeness existed between the paper and

making

me, ~~It is~~ a very pleasant and private emotional experience.

On the other hand, having to concern myself with punctuation and

effective   *has slowed*

~~proper~~ sentence structure really ~~slows~~ me down. Not only do I hesitate

to begin writing, I also don't know what to write about or even how to

say it. Sometimes I get frustrated because while I wait for my pen to

give me the words I am searching for, my pen waits for me. The word

"clause" has brought new meaning to my life, because in the past it had

only represented one thing—the little fat man who brought toys to our

Now it brings up images of connectors and punctuation marks.

home at Christmas. ~~However,~~ I do find that the process of writing I'm

learning is so radically different from my carefree way of attacking the page that ~~its~~ *it is* a challenge I enjoy. Although it is difficult to write for a

critical reader, I get excited when I complete a paper that I have edited

and revised several times ⊙ *At that point* ~~because~~ I know my sentences are more

concise and my words more clearly state my thoughts.

When I wrote for myself, I only wrote it once, *and never made corrections or* When I reread those *changes.*

pages, I am thankful that I had the sense to take this writing course,

because I am learning how to make the pages speak my thoughts better

than I ever thought ~~imagined was~~ possible.

Writing for Myself or Others

I've enjoyed writing all my life, but since I began this composition class, I've had much difficulty putting my pen to paper. It was much easier writing only for myself, because then I did not have to worry about using proper grammar or an effective style for someone else's benefit.

Before I took this course, I would write only for me. My only concern was to capture my private thoughts and feelings. I would take my pen in hand, get some paper, and write. The pen in my hand would glide across the page leaving a message from my soul. The time passed quickly and the pages filled fast. I always felt an attraction to the empty page. I was never at a loss for words. A sense of kinship and closeness existed between the paper and me, making a very pleasant and private emotional experience.

On the other hand, having to concern myself with punctuation and effective sentence structure really has slowed me down. Not only do I hesitate to begin writing, I also don't know what to write about or even how to say it. Sometimes I get frustrated because while I wait for my pen to give me the words I am searching for, my pen waits for me. The word "clause" has brought new meaning to my life, because in the past it had only represented one thing—the little fat man who brought toys to our home at Christmas. Now it brings up images of connectors and punctuation marks. However, I do find that the process of writing I'm learning is so radically different from my carefree way of attacking the page that it is a challenge I enjoy. Although it is difficult to write for a critical reader, I get excited when I complete a paper that I have edited and revised several times. At that point I know my sentences are more concise and my words more clearly state my thoughts.

When I wrote for myself, I only wrote it once and never made corrections or changes. When I reread those pages, I am thankful that I had the sense to take this writing course, because I am learning how to make the pages speak my thoughts better than I ever thought possible.

For Discussion

1. How does the revision of Maryellyn's first sentence emphasize the comparison and contrast nature of this essay?
2. Does this essay follow the part-by-part or the whole-by-whole method of development? (see pages 139–141 for review)
3. What transition markers does Maryellyn use to move from one paragraph to the next? How does the wording of these markers also help emphasize comparison and contrast?
4. What ideas from the two body paragraphs are summarized in the conclusion?

WRITING YOUR OWN COMPARISON AND CONTRAST ESSAY

Exercise 1

In the two columns below list similar and contrasting facts about your generation and your parents' generation. Keep your listing parallel. List a fact about your generation and across the page the balancing fact about your parents' generation. List as many as you can think of.

my generation	my parents' generation
1. _____	1. _____
2. _____	2. _____
3. _____	3. _____
4. _____	4. _____
5. _____	5. _____
6. _____	6. _____
7. _____	7. _____
8. _____	8. _____
9. _____	9. _____
10. _____	10. _____
11. _____	11. _____
12. _____	12. _____

You probably made your list randomly, just as ideas came to your mind. Now you have to go through your list and classify as many of the items as possible into broad categories. You are given one such category below. List whatever others seem appropriate, and beneath each broad category place the specific items from your list.

attitudes toward sex
_____

   specific items:

_____

   specific items:

_____

   specific items:

_____
specific items:

Select several items that you have listed to point up similarities between the two generations. Write a topic sentence for a paragraph that would use these items and treat only similarities. Include a reference to the items in your topic sentence.

Would you organize such a paragraph according to plan A or plan B? Explain why you think your choice would be the more effective one.

Select several items that you have listed to point up differences between the two generations. Write a topic sentence for a paragraph that would use these items and treat only differences. Include a reference to the items in your topic sentence.

Would you organize such a paragraph according to plan A or plan B? Explain why you think your choice would be the more effective one.

Write one of the paragraphs that you discussed above. First present a brief outline for your paragraph below to indicate your method of organization.

One frequently used method for organizing your essay of comparison and contrast is first to look at the ways in which the objects are similar and then to examine the ways in which they are different. Such an organizational scheme is most often followed by a conclusion that makes some type of summary evaluation of the objects. The body of your essay might have an organization much like the following:

items that are similar

my parents' generation   **at least one**
  (specific details)   **paragraph**

my generation   **at least one**
  (specific details)   **paragraph**

items that are different

my parents' generation   **at least one**
  (specific details)   **paragraph**

my generation   **at least one**
  (specific details)   **paragraph**

When you frame this type of outline with an introduction and a conclusion, you have a complete working scheme for a fully developed essay.

Use an organizational scheme similar to the one above to develop your own essay on the similarities and differences between your generation and your parents' generation. Let your thesis sentence indicate that you will be writing about both similarities and differences. Your conclusion should make an evaluation about the two generations.

Exercise 2

Develop a second comparison and contrast essay based on one of the topics listed below. You might want to use a working system similar to the one you just used with the two different generations to get your ideas going and to sort them into meaningful categories.

attending a community college and attending a state university
two movies (of similar type) that you have recently seen
two politicians and their plans for the future
the life-styles in two different cities or neighborhoods

C H A P T E R

12

Process Analysis

Usually you write directions or instructions for a very limited situation and you need no more than one fully developed paragraph to present all of the necessary information. Occasionally, however, the process you are describing is so complicated that you have to expand your writing to several paragraphs of explanation. If you think your readers might be tempted to skip over one step entirely, you might include specific information about why that step is so important, even suggesting the bad things that might happen if it is skipped. If you know the most common mistakes made by individuals who attempt this process, you might do as the sample essay below does and present a paragraph focusing solely on things not to do. Each step or each major time block of action is usually organized into a separate paragraph and developed with appropriate detail and explanation. *For a review of the basic organizational principles of process analysis, you might want to reread pages 146–148.*

A PROCESS ANALYSIS ESSAY

Here are the rough draft and final versions of Kim's essay on how to stencil a wooden cheesebox. Carefully read both versions of the essay to see what changes she made in the final one so that it would be a more effective set of directions.

By decorating a colorful stenciled cheesebox, you can create a conversational piece that is not only attractive but useful as well! It can be used as a sewing kit, a storage box for edibles, or anything else you wish. Because the preparation for the stenciling can be a little involved, you need to start gathering your materials. You will need a round wooden cheesebox (unpainted), fine grained sandpaper, a pad of steel wool, several small jars of paint (colors of your choice), stencils of whatever motif you wish, a container of water, a two-inch paintbrush, masking tape, paper towels, a tack cloth, and a can of spray acrylic-lacquer.

Before you begin, perhaps I should explain what not to do so you will be able to move along at a steady pace. Do not paint the box until you first use a tack cloth to remove the dust from sanding. When the stencil is placed around the sides of cheesebox or on the lid, be sure not to move to the other because the paint will bleed under the cut stencil and run into the colors. Do not use the steel wool until the paint is completely dried.

The first thing you need to do is thoroughly sand the top and sides of the cheesebox, wiping it completely with a tack cloth so there is not any dirt from the sanding left on it. Now you are ready to paint your first coat of paint on the box; you may choose any color. Be sure to paint in only one direction with the brush so you will not cause streaking. Wait until that coat is dry and add another coat of the same color. Two coats are preferable because when the steel wool's used it will not scrape paint to get the antique effect off entirely to the wood grain. ~~Now that~~ *When* the box is dry, steel wool can be

gently and lightly brushed *in one direction only* across the sides and lid to create an antique

look. ~~Be sure to brush the steel wool in one direction only.~~

Next, ~~At this time~~, you are ready to ~~afix~~ *place* your stencil onto the cheesebox .

~~using any type of motif you choose.~~ You need to make sure the stencil is

placed firmly against the box with the covers at each end of the stencil

sheet secured with the masking tape. The reason for this is *that* if the stencil

sheet moves or *gets* jarred, the area painted can be ruined by *the* paint bleeding *and smearing the design or giving it a blotched affect*

into other colors or running under the plastic stencil sheet.

Now is the time for you to choose any colors you want to decorate

your cheesebox, being sure to completely clean your brush each time to

keep the colors pure.

After you have decided that you are finished and have applied

enough *stenciling* ~~stencils~~ on your cheesebox, let *the paint twenty-four* set for ~~24~~ hours. At all times

make sure your work area is clean.

The last step requires you to spray acrylic-lacquer *on* ~~to~~ the box. Be

sure to hold the can with the nozzle facing the box, *and six inches* approximately ~~8"~~

from it. *Using an* ~~In~~ even swaying motion ~~with~~ *of* your hand, keep *the* nozzle depressed

and coat sides and lid of box evenly and wait *twenty-four* ~~24~~ hours, *for the lacquer* to dry.

When you have finished, your ~~The~~ end product is a hand-made craft that can be ~~handed~~ *passed* down

through the family and used for anything you wish. It is *Now* valuable, *and* with the

spray finish on it ~~and~~ can fit into any decor.

By decorating a colorful stenciled cheesebox, you can create a conversational piece that is not only attractive but useful as well. It can be used as a sewing kit, a storage box for edibles, or anything else you wish.

Because the preparation for the stenciling can be a little involved, you need to start gathering your materials. You will need a round wooden cheesebox (unpainted), fine grained sandpaper, a pad of steel wool, several small jars of paint (colors of your choice), stencils of whatever motif you wish, a container of water, a two-inch paintbrush, masking tape, paper towels, a tack cloth, and a can of spray acrylic-lacquer.

Before you begin, perhaps I should explain what not to do so you will be able to move along at a steady pace. Do not paint the box until you first use a tack cloth to remove the dust from your sanding. When the stencil is placed around the sides of the cheesebox or on the lid, be sure not to move it because the paint will bleed under the cut stencil and run into other colors. Do not use the steel wool until the paint has completely dried.

The first thing you need to do is thoroughly sand the top and sides of the cheesebox, wiping it completely with a tack cloth so there is no dirt from the sanding left on it.

Now you are ready to paint your first coat of paint on the box; you may choose any color. Be sure to paint in only one direction with the brush so you will not cause streaking. Wait until that coat is dry and add another coat of the same color. Two coats are preferable because when the steel wool is used to get the antique effect, it will not scrape paint off entirely to the wood grain. When the box is dry, the steel wool can be gently and lightly brushed in one direction only across the sides and lid to create an antique look.

Next, you are ready to place your stencil onto the cheesebox. You need to make sure the stencil is placed firmly against the box with the covers at each end of the stencil sheet secured with the masking tape. The reason for this is that if the stencil sheet moves or gets jarred, the area painted can be ruined by paint bleeding into other colors or running under the plastic stencil sheet and smearing the design or giving it a blotched effect.

Now is the time for you to choose any colors you want to decorate your cheesebox, being sure to completely clean your brush each time to keep the colors pure.

After you have decided that you are finished and have applied enough stenciling on your cheesebox, let the paint set for twenty-four hours. Even then make sure your work area is clean.

The last step requires you to spray acrylic-lacquer on the box. Be sure to hold the can with the nozzle facing the box and approximately six inches from it. Using an even swaying motion of your hand, keep the nozzle depressed and coat the sides and lid of box evenly and wait twenty-four hours for the lacquer to dry.

When you have finished, your end product is a hand-made craft that can be handed down through the family and used for anything you wish. It is now valuable and with the spray finish on it can fit into any decor.

For Discussion

1. In her revised version of this essay, Kim has changed the word *we* to *you* in several places. What is the effect of this change? If Kim addresses her reader as *you*, is she still justified in using *I* to refer to herself?
2. The purpose of the first body paragraph is to let the reader know what supplies are necessary for this task. Do you think that it is a good idea to list the supplies in a separate paragraph like this, or would it be just as effective to mention each different item at the point in the process when it is to be used?
3. What do you think about Kim's separate paragraph on things not to do? Is it effective? Why do you think she put it at this position in the paper and not at the end of the paper?
4. What transitional words does Kim use to move from one step in the process to the next? How does she avoid repeating the same words over and over until they become boring?
5. In what way does her conclusion complete her introduction? What similar ideas are in each?

WRITING YOUR OWN PROCESS ANALYSIS ESSAY

The introduction to a process analysis essay depends less on an attention device than does the introduction for most of the other modes.

When you are writing about how to do something, you generally assume that your readers are interested in the task and that you should simply explain the process in a businesslike manner.

If you do feel that you need to do something dramatic to get your readers' attention, one of the best ways is to explain how knowing and using the process that you are discussing will help them personally. For instance, if you are presenting a detailed set of instructions on how to tune an automobile, you might first begin with some indication of why the task is important or worthwhile:

> It continues to amaze me that so many people drive around with poorly tuned automobile engines. According to one recent survey, at least seven out of every ten cars on the road were in need of a tune-up. That same survey pointed out that a well-tuned engine could get about one-third more miles per gallon of gasoline. If you want to save all of that gasoline money and get your engine tuned for less than twenty dollars, all you have to do is follow these easy directions.

This essay would then treat each step of the process—changing spark plugs, changing and adjusting points, adjusting timing, and so on—in a separate paragraph. The conclusion of the essay would probably tie the entire process back to the concern for saving money that was discussed in the introduction.

> The choices are really rather simple. You can continue to watch a third of your gasoline money go out in gray-blue exhaust fumes, you can take your automobile to a garage and spend close to a hundred dollars for a tune-up, or you can follow these steps and do it yourself for no more than one tank of gas would cost.

Exercise 1

Assume that someone you don't know is going to take your place at work for an entire day. If you do not work, assume that someone you don't know is going to take your place at home and school for an entire day. Prepare an essay that will serve as a kind of instruction manual for this individual. Begin by completing the following scheme of important information that you will want to work into your report:

Where to go:

Time to report:

Equipment/supplies to bring:

People to meet:

Specific duties to perform:

Location of necessary supplies, forms, etc.:

Now, prepare a step-by-step chronological sequence of activities that will take the individual through every phase of the day. Significant changes in tasks to perform or in time slots will mark the beginnings of new paragraphs.

Exercise 2

Develop a process analysis essay on one of the topics listed below. For whatever topic you select, assume that you are the expert and that your reader is only casually familiar with it.

how to make an *A* in this English class (or any other class you are currently taking)
how to apply for financial aid
how to give cardio-pulmonary resuscitation
how to lose weight (or stop smoking or stop drinking)

C H A P T E R

13

Causal Analysis

Your multiparagraph essay should clearly identify a result or final effect and then carefully examine the causes that led to it. Depending upon your purpose, the essay might also propose some solutions to the problem(s) that you have analyzed. *For a review of the basic organizational principles of causal analysis, you might want to reread pages 152–158.*

A CAUSAL ANALYSIS ESSAY

John wrote the essay below in response to an assignment that asked him to analyze the decision in his life which had caused him the most personal frustration. Notice how he begins his essay by identifying the result that he is going to analyze. He then looks at each contributing cause in a separate paragraph. His essay ends with the solution that he found to his problem.

Living on my own made me realize how dependent I am on my *of my eighteenth birthday* family. The day ~~I turned eighteen~~ I thought I was ~~able to take care of~~ *mature enough to leave home* ~~myself so I opted to live on my own.~~ ~~To my parents' surprise and anger I~~ *that I was to share* ~~was committed to live on my own~~ I found a house ~~to live in that~~ three *with friends of mine. I gathered my things and moved into* ~~other guys shared.~~ The deal for me was that I live in the basement in a *my "new home,"* *where I lived in the*

many problems that made me question my initial decision

my three friends and I would split the

small room which provided ^privacy. ~~a separate room and I pay the~~ rent equally.

After moving my belongings and settling in, I noticed ~~some diff for a few days I felt my living style was quite different than that of home.~~ ¶ My first problem was not coming home to a hot meal.

♪ When I came home at nights, I didn't find dinner being kept warm in the oven. If I wanted anything to eat, I either made it myself or went out to eat. ~~instead I had to make it myself.~~ I didn't ^eat very nutritional ~~have a consistent set of foods ever~~ at my new place. ~~I often ate unnutritional foods.~~ Along with finding something to eat, ~~if I wanted to eat I had to take money out of my check and save it for grocery money. Along with insufficient food,~~ I had to plan ahead to pay for it, whether I ate at home or went out. I had to realize that my mom wasn't there to cook and care for me. Another problem was keeping up ~~my clothes weren't as clean as they often are.~~ with the laundry. I wasn't as skilled with the laundry as my mom was. I would often wear the same pants for a [reverse order] And when I did wash, clothes never came out really clean. ¶ week just so I didn't have to wash so often. ~~In addition to coping with providing adequate food and clean clothes,~~ Aside from eating a lot of peanut butter sandwiches and wearing slightly dirty clothes, I also had to clean my living area. I did many things for the first time, like dusting, vacuuming, and washing walls ~~I had to keep up the cleaning or my room would look~~ I wanted my room to look good and not ^like a junk yard. I had to realize that I didn't have mommy to pick up after me. ^I slowly came to realize how much ~~After encountering these things for the first time I asked myself if I really~~ of what happened at home I had taken for ~~was ready to live on my own. Another problem was lineliness,~~ granted. ^By this time I had also begun to feel Although I very lonely in my new quarters.

shared a house with three other good friends, I was usually by myself. I had other friends over quite a bit, but still there was a sense of loneliness. I missed my family. After living on my own for almost two months, I ~~decided go back home for a combination of reasons~~ realized several things. First of all, I ~~realized~~ decided that I wasn't as mature as I thought ~~I was to live on my own~~ just because I was eighteen. Second, ~~I felt that by living on my own away from the family I might regret.~~ I am better off with my family than on my own right now. ~~Last of all, I wanted to be stable because school was coming up and I didn't think I would succeed if still living on my own.~~ Finally, this whole experience made me realize how selfish I was and that I had neglected a family that loves me.

Living on my own made me realize how dependent I am on my family. The day of my eighteenth birthday I thought I was mature enough to leave home. I found a house that I was to share with three friends of mine. I gathered my things and moved into my "new home," where I lived in the basement in a small room which provided privacy. My friends and I would split the rent equally. After moving my belongings and settling in, I noticed many problems that made me question my initial decison.

My first problem was not coming home to a hot meal. When I came home at night, I didn't find dinner being kept warm in the oven. If I wanted anything to eat, I either made it myself or went out to eat. I didn't eat very nutritional foods at my new place. Along with finding something to eat, I had to plan ahead to pay for it, whether I ate at home or went out.

Another problem was keeping up with the laundry. I would often wear the same pants for a week just so I didn't have to wash so often. And when I did wash, clothes never came out really clean. I wasn't as skilled with the laundry as my mom was.

Aside from eating a lot of peanut butter sandwiches and wearing slightly dirty clothes, I had to clean my living area. I did many things like dusting, vacuuming, and washing walls for the first time. I wanted my room to look good and not like a junk yard. I had to realize that I didn't have Mommy to pick up after me.

By this time I had also begun to feel very lonely in my new quarters. Although I shared a house with three good friends, I was usually by myself. I had other friends over quite a bit, but still there was a sense of loneliness. I missed my family.

After living on my own for almost two months, I realized several things. First of all, I decided that I wasn't as mature as I thought just because I was eighteen. Second, I am better off with my family than on my own right now. Finally, this whole experience made me realize how selfish I was and that I had neglected a family that loves me.

For Discussion

1. Carefully study the first paragraph in John's rough draft and in his final essay. How has he rewritten that final version so it more clearly sets the essay up to analyze a problem?
2. What effect do you think John was trying to achieve in moving from the word *mom* in the second paragraph to *Mommy* in the third?
3. Why do you suppose John completely changed the final sentence of his fourth paragraph? Why is the ending to this paragraph in the final version better?
4. John almost completely rewrote the conclusion when he did his final version of this essay. Compare the two conclusions. What are the differences in purpose between the two?

WRITING YOUR OWN CAUSAL ANALYSIS ESSAY

Exercise 1

Work from the same writing assignment that John used for his essay. Think of a decision in your life that has caused you much personal frustration and then think about what you learned from both that decision and that frustration. You might want to look once more at the structure of John's essay, paying particular attention to what he does in his introduction and conclusion, and structure your own essay in a similar manner.

Exercise 2

Causal analysis can very quickly become extremely complicated and long. It can also become highly controversial. Failure to agree on major issues of causal analysis, for instance, is what frequently separates Democrats and Republicans or the American Cancer Society and the tobacco industry.

When discussing or writing about highly complicated issues (effects), you will often find it impossible to discuss every cause; your analysis would become much too lengthy and complicated. Rather, you attempt to identify the major causes and to combine or classify some of the minor causes under one broad heading.

For your essay, select one of the issues listed below or an issue of your own choice that is equally complicated and controversial:

racial injustice in the United States
rapidly increasing inflation in the United States
increasing crime rate in the United States
the shift of political attitudes in the United States (from liberal to conservative, for instance).

In the space below, list at least fifteen causes, as you see them, for the effect that you are analyzing.

1. _____

2. _____

3. _____

4. _____

5. _____

6. _____

7. _____

8. _____

9. _____

10. _____

11. _____

12. _____

13. _____

14. _____

15. _____

Compare your list with ones prepared by your classmates. See if it is possible to produce a list that is generally similar. Attempt to eliminate from your list the minor or local causes and focus on the five or six major ones that you have identified.

In the spaces below, arrange your list according to chronological order and order of increasing importance.

chronological order   **order of increasing importance**

_____   _____

_____   _____

_____   _____

_____   _____

_____   _____

_____   _____

_____   _____

_____   _____

_____   _____

Which system of order do you think will be the most effective for your finished essay?

_____

Why?

_____

_____

Using the ordering system that you have selected, write your finished essay. Be certain to indicate in your thesis sentence that you are discussing only the *major* causes and not *all* of the causes. Develop each individual cause into one or more paragraphs.

Exercise 3

Your task in the essay assignment you just completed was to analyze causes and not to offer solutions. It is only logical that you first identify the causes of a problem before you set out to correct the problem.

Look back at the causes that you have identified in the essay. What solutions do you see? Recalling what you learned in the earlier section on process analysis, write an essay in which you present your suggestions for solving the problems (causes) that you have identified.

Index